# The Dicey Problem of New Age Science

## Einstein, Hawking and God at the Casino

Dwaraknath Reddy

# The Dicey Problem of New Age Science

## Einstein, Hawking and God at the Casino

Dwaraknath Reddy

# Appreciation

*Elevating, thought-provoking and delightful from the points of view of spirituality, science, and literature.... While enriching parallels between science and spirituality, Reddy's book all the same faces the scientist squarely. His poser on consciousness: Is brain the powerhouse, or the power source?...... Get the answer right, for Reality revolves on that pivot.*

*– **Swami Chidananda** (physicist and scholar)*
*Earlier, Chief Acharya of Chinmaya Mission;*
*Later, Director, Chinmaya International*
*Foundation,Cochin.*

*Excellent book.... Grippingly tight script in impeccable idiom reveals the creative mind of the intellectual and spiritual author.... leads the reader from origins of the universe, through the limitations of science, to prior and pervading Consciousness (like electromagnetic field that fills the universe).*

*– **Dr. K. Srinivasa Rao**, FNAsc.,*
*Senior Professor (Retd.),*
*The Institute of Mathematical Sciences, Chennai*

# Comments on earlier writings by the same author:

*Here we have an artist at work, an artist who is a scientist by education and a mystic by accomplishment. This singular combination sets the book apart.... A gifted writer... with a style that is precise and incisive.... able to drive home subtle points in a few vibrant words. His keen sense of humour makes the entire work lively and spiced with witty 'asides' and whispered sarcasm... A very enjoyable and invigorating experience for me to read him.*

*– **Swami Iswarananda Giri** (Vedantic scholar and saint.)*
*Mount Abu, Rajasthan.*

*"Chiselled expressions of the intricate beauty of his soaring thoughts.... each chapter an upanishadic canto...."*

*– **Swami Chinmayananda***
*(Internationally acclaimed exponent of vedanta, and spiritual master.)*

*"One line, one thought, and it is enough to drive one to contemplation.... a book to be savoured, not swallowed."*

*– **M.V. Kamath** (Nationally acclaimed intellecual)*
*Bhavan's Journal, Bombay.*

*"The approach is both scholarly and mystic. Pages soaked with fundamental upanishadic ideas regarding mind, consciousness, ego, along with concepts of Relativity and quantum physics... scintillating lines... clarity of vision of author's flight on two wings of reason and intuition."*

*– **Swami Jitatmananda** (Physicist, turned senior monk.)*
*Sri Ramakrishna Mission, Rajkot.*

*".....reproducible reliable subjective experiences also can be communicated and evoked. Dwaraknath Reddy shows us by example how this can be done. I am pleased to introduce this book to the scientific spirit of enquiry in all of you, professional scientist and layman alike."*

*– **Dr. E.C.G. Sudarshan,** (Reputed Maths-science professor)*
*University of Texas, Austin, USA.*

*Marvellous book... the spiritual personality of the author unfolds in an extraordinary manner... a treasure... profound ideas conveyed with rare skill effortlessly.*

*– **The Hindu,** Leading National Daily*

*"A humanist? word-artist? Seeker of Truth? Reddy is all and more. Beauty of style and power of thought... authenticity of experience.... precision of expression...."*

*– **M.P. Pandit** (Author, Scholar, and Teacher)*
*Sri Aurobindo Ashram, Pondicherry.*

# About the Author

He was already thirty-five when a tragic event raised haunting questions about creation and creator, about order or chance decreeing birth and death, and about ultimate meanings and methods in all our lives. Could there be in creation an overall unfolding cosmic purpose? Perhaps not, said his rational mind. But that answer would have to be the final conclusion of diligent enquiry, it would not be the first dogma of furious frustration.

A' 48 batch post-graduate in Science from Louisiana State University (USA), he joined his father in starting a modest food processing unit, which he built up gradually into the largest in India in that industry. Prosperity, prestige and recognition became the outer facade of success. The inner urge to seek and resolve his rightful place in creation remained the focus of his life.

With no traditional training or exposure to philosophy till then, he listened, studied, contemplated, and alertly remained concerned. Openness and earnestness were his only assets, but they were enough to gain step after step an unravelling of the answers with objective clarity and linked logic.

However, objective knowledge is a science learnt, not a science lived. One learns physics, biology, economics, history and the knowledge serves utilitarian purposes. But knowledge of oneself, the deeper significance of "know thyself", has to be subjective. It is not to serve a need, but to place one beyond need. What could be more challenging, or rewarding?

Dwaraknath Reddy stays and strives on that path. When he came across the teachings of Ramana Maharshi, unfolding the nuances of Self-Enquiry, focussed on the core question "WHO AM I?", he was flooded with an inner conviction that Ramana Maharshi was the epitome of all scriptures and their promise to humanity of attainable perfection. Therefore, for strength and comfort in his chosen pursuit, Reddy lives in the sanctified sanctuary of Sri Ramanashramam, Tiruvannamalai, S. India (TN 606 603). While walking towards a cherished destination, every step is pure delight. He remains a seeker.

Other Books by Dwaraknath Reddy

- Can God Improve My Balance Sheet?
- Diving Deep into Ramana Maharshi's Teachings
- Death Was Never Born Life Never Died
- The Physics of Karma
- Gentle Breeze, Rustling Leaves
- Rising Sun Melting Mists
- Divya, The Rainbow Child
- Sumangali

*'God does not play dice.'*
*Einstein*


*'God is quite a gambler.'*
*Stephen Hawking*

# CONTENTS

SUPPLEMENT: CONTENTS



- Modern physics says time began with the Big Bang.
- Bio-science says mind is a product of brain-cells.
- Philosophy has always said that Consciousness is eternal.
- A holistic study of these statements is possible.
- Such study is essential to understand creation and creator.

The Personified proof of the promise of transcendence
that the Absolute holds out to the relative.

# Preface To The Second (Enlarged) Edition

When a reprint of this book was being considered, I came across "Quantum Questions" by Ken Wilber, in which, through personal comment and compilation, he has created a volume that for me was deeply and delightfully relevant. My book had been written addressing the physicist and the bio-scientist, with acceptance of and admiration for their analyses and insights into cosmic energies and molecular evolution, while simultaneously stating for their consideration, or reconsideration, that, within the disciplines of their linked and linear rationale, the reference to the First Factor, or Creator, or Beginning, or the Thing-in-itself, or the Unified Field, or the Theory-of-Everything, could not even be adequately formulated – how then could it be answered? Wrong questions elicit wrong answers.

So it was refreshing that Ken Wilber put scientific conclusions in right perspective, and brought to our ears and minds a chorus of voices, his own included, of brilliant men of science, who never claimed to be saying the last word but said distinctly that quantum physics did not reduce or blur – how then, eliminate? – the division between the subjective and the objective. To think so involved a misuse of language. An honest assertion. And the perfect jumping-board to dive into the very words "subjective and objective," till we can set apart the subject from the object, the perceiver from the perceived, the knower from the known.

I found myself in debt to Ken Wilber for his summary of Eddington's precise analysis that "the exploration of the external world by the method of physical science leads not to a concrete reality, but to a shadow world of symbols. To penetrate beyond, we return to *human consciousness....*"

The core purpose of my writing has been to lay relentless stress on "consciousness". If this is a factor in the processes of matter – by which we mean, if consciousness is a product of neural chemistry – then it too is one of the symbols that science is already familiar with. There can be no penetrating beyond.

If in saying that we place upon ourselves a self-imposed limitation, we defeat and frustrate ourselves. The solution lies in re-examining the potency of our tools, which are words (symbols). Let us find the words to understand the word "word", for without words there is no mentation. Then let us see what opens up.

Let us not take comfort in soothing phrases. If "science is blind without religion, and religion is lame without science," creeping about individually both will fall into pits individually. If they team-up piggy-back and march together, both will still fall into the pit of limitation together. Take your choice.

Ken Wilber's precise, pertinent, and probing questions pushed me deeper into my contemplations. As a result, I felt motivated and empowered. The clarity of his questions invoked clarity of mental response in my search. Gratefully and joyously I have added a few chapters to the first edition and feel a deeper sense of fulfilment.

At this point of time another book "From Science to God" by Peter Russell (Publisher: Yogi Impressions) has come to my hands. I have benefited from the reading, and have felt propelled to look deeper into the significance of the word "Light" in "terrestrial" and "celestial" connotations. I have now included in my book the extension of the train of thought initiated upon reading Peter Russell. Light which facilitates material perception is "gross". The "light of knowledge" that facilitates mental responses is "subtle" by comparison, it is the pointer to consciousness. When the word "knowledge" is subjected to scrutiny and seen in the context of cosmic manifestation, it stands exposed as just another aspect of relativity, in which frame of reference our knowledge (the known) and our ignorance (as yet unknown) add up to be the twins born of a primal descent from the Absolute to the relative, from Absolute Reality to a relative reality, from Light to reflected light. At that level primary "light" denotes its "causal" state. Words here are demanding our deeper probe; they cannot be abandoned, as they are the only tools of the intellect. Hone the tools, sharpen them, and we will find them adequate for the task. They can cut the ropes that bind thought.

---

Third edition includes a new supplement.
*Please see page 131.*

Towards the end of 2007, I came across a book by Mani Bhaumik of "Laser" renown, a physicist and spiritual seeker. The book "Code name God" is an intelligent, informative and illuminating probe on the physics/philosophy border, an area of the deepest relevance to my own spiritual contemplations. I found that some thoughts of Dr. Bhaumik could be corelated, compared or contrasted purposefully and profitably with what I had written in my book "The Dicey Problem of New Age Science". Therefore I wrote a supplement to be included in the third edition of my book.

This development is further elaborated in the chapter "Code name God – author's name Mani Bhaumik", which is the first of the added chapters in this edition.

*Dwaraknath Reddy*
December 2008.

# Preamble: The Great Divide

Early in January, 2001, some of the world's leading physicists gathered in India to discuss the findings and problems of their discipline centred in particle physics. Why is the universe the way it is? How did it get there? And where is it going? These were some of the basic questions to be answered.

Amongst the celebrities, and deservedly acknowledged not only as a scholar of rare genius, but also as a legendary symbol of human courage, endurance and determination, was Dr. Stephen Hawking. Around 1963, then only twenty-one years old, he was diagnosed as a victim of an incurable disease affecting the nerves responsible for movement. The progressive malady, doctors said, would end his life in a couple of years. Yet, with a wasted body, confined to a wheelchair, deprived of the ability to speak and compelled to articulate the inward flashes of his transcendental intellect only through computer wizardry, Dr. Hawking is blazing new trails in physics and allied mathematics.

Naturally, media attention was focussed on the conference. Even laymen were willing to labour through a para or two of quarks and quantum mechanics, if only to feel thereby some proximity to the one-and-only Hawking. The great man's quotes were choicest banner headlines.

So on January 12 I was looking at the bold print in The Hindu, the widely-acclaimed national newspaper, that proclaimed the even bolder statement, "GOD PLAYED DICE WITH UNIVERSE: HAWKING". The prelude was also highlighted in the article, that Einstein, the other mighty stalwart of science, had, in the developing context, earlier expressed his opinion "GOD DOES NOT PLAY DICE". In fact, Hawking was saying that the scientific concept of matter was shifting from the theory of relativity to quantum theory with its probability functions.

Why was GOD made a party to the dispute?

Neither statement was made lightly nor in jest. Both these scientists are amongst the greatest physicists who have revolutionized concepts of time, space, causal determinism, and energy functions. They are applying their ascending understanding of the spectrum of knowledge stretching from cosmic origins at the macro-level to atomic structuring at the micro-level, and sensing a shift from the rigid chanceless determinism of Newtonian physical laws, to the flexible probability functions of quantum mechanics.

Though sounding as if spoken in a lighter vein, both the statements actually connote the essence of the perceptions of these two great intellects on the creation of the universe. Their findings are based on acute observation, experimentation, and analysis. Einstein was not inclined to accept that, whatever may be the scheme of energy-play accounting for creation (as we know creation), it could be determined by the toss of a coin (or the throw of a dice). There could not be the element of chance. And Einstein with his personal conviction that 'God is subtle but not malicious', would not have been averse to using the word GOD for the creative energy, though the physicist in him had no need for that word in the given scientific context. He was not starting a theological argument. He would rather uphold the concept of a reliable God who reveals himself in the harmony of what exists (the God of Spinoza).

Stephen Hawking was convinced that chance (meaning probability) remains the supreme arbiter of what is, was, and will be. That was the law. And if Einstein had posited a law-maker in the word GOD, it was fun to go along with the same idiom and say that his GOD was shown up as a gambler. I may be mistaken (and will be glad if I am) but Hawking has no sympathy with a dicey divine parading as a paragon, and would rather put him in his place (could it be a Black Hole?) by laying bare the "mind of god".

With both, "GOD" was a fleeting digression. It was not meant to be physics. But the inclusion of the "observer" as an interwoven factor in the description of the "observed", brought the element of consciousness into the reckoning, for, an observer is instinctively read as a conscious person. If science is discussing energy-fields and invites a reference to consciousness, then science must, in all decency, listen to another breed of "scientists" that have explored and explained an energy-field that includes and exceeds the energies known to science, which are gravity, electro-magnetic forces, radiation, etc., – *the energy-field of consciousness*. This field was propounded and formulated by the scientists of Life. We call them sages and seers. They have been there since ages and ages past, and in many climes and countries.

They are with us today too, sung and unsung. Theirs always was the science of the energy-system that moved thought-particles in the knowledge-field. Time, Space and Causation were the relevant factors in their reckoning too. And so was the observer. There could be no ambiguity about the theme they were propounding with analytical precision, for they called it *"Kshetra and Kshetrajna"*, which translates into "Field and the Knower of the Field." The sages arrived, each one individually, at Reality in Creation, in terms far exceeding external perception; in terms of inner personal experience. It could all be communicated and others could repeat the process and progress in themselves and thus validate the truth of the statements. When thus realized, Reality was always the same.

Is that not science?

The seers have a word to indicate that Reality. Their word is GOD.

Scientists have to have a word too for the goal of their quest. They do not concede that beyond scientific experiment and verification, anyone can claim to convey or express Reality. The sage can only have an opinion or an illusion (hoping it is not pretence). Science alone is precise, and the frontiers of knowledge are expanding. Recently, scientists say, they have arrived at the knowledge of DNA. The new insights into what seems to be the deciding and controlling system behind the forms and behavioural patterns of living organisms, and the promise held therein for a complete resolution of the mystery of life, seem to have filled more authentically the void in scientific knowledge that the god of easy believers had hijacked. As of now, their preferred word for a pointer to Reality is perhaps DNA.

Reading what the newspapers were highlighting, and a bemused audience was innocently applauding, I could not hold back a call for intervention. Never mind if my contribution would most likely end up in the wastepaper basket of the editorial office. (They must be keeping extra-large ones to accommodate people like me.) I felt I had something relevant to say on the subject, eked out from the time-honoured teachings of my ancient land. I had a respectful but proud submission to make, without offending the tenor of science for linked and logical rationale. So I wrote a brief article and sent it to *The Hindu.* They published it. Thank you *Hindu*!

The article dealt with limited consciousness as possessed and experienced by the individual (you and me), and as it may be projected and postulated in terms of the totality of consciousness; and explained how the two frames stood in relation to each other, as numbers to infinity, as reflections to a subject, as relativity to Absolutism. Total consciousness, the Infinite Absolute Reality, had been given the word-symbol GOD. The limited got the name MAN.

And now it was time to fit myself into the indulgent banter of the scientists at the casino of creation; so I wrote, *inter alia,* "Please do not waste your sympathy upon Absolute Consciousness, the Creator, by wanting to feel reassured that God does not play dice, while your observations indicate that He seems to be doing just that. Do not worry about Him for He remains at the same time the absolute owner of the casino. When He plays, His left hand picks up what the right hand loses. His status remains unaltered. We had better be looking out for ourselves."

The thrust of the argument was this: Scientific investigation of reality progresses from speculation to experiment to observation. Ideas thus get rejected or accepted, and in course of time what was accepted earlier is abandoned and new concepts hold sway. Such perforce has to be the march of knowledge. We, the conscious individuals, are playing the dice in the casino of objective knowledge, lacking secure observation-posts outside. We are within the four walls of relativity. The Absolute includes and exceeds all of relativity. If you posit a Creator, His fulcrum is beyond the relative and He can lever out creation. We cannot do that from our perch within relativity. He is the master of the casino and the director of the play.

The article raised a few ripples, for I received some approving and appreciative letters from readers. Now chance took a strangely lucky turn – a gamble that paid off? Dr. B. Ramamurthi of Chennai (Madras) is a neurosurgeon nationally renowned for decades. Over ninety, he is alert and active, practising, and committed to his science and profession. He is the chairman of the National Brain Research Centre of India (NBRC.) He read the article and graciously took the trouble to write to me (an unknown) a personal letter. He said "I want to congratulate you on the lucidity of the article and the great ideas you have clearly explained."

It happened that NBRC, in association with the Computer Society of India, and endorsed by the Institute of Mathematical Sciences (Chennai), had already programmed a conference to be held in Chennai in just a couple of weeks. The theme was "CONSCIOUS 2001, conference on FACETS OF CONSCIOUSNESS". The stated goal was to discuss and understand the "basic mechanisms of consciousness as each group (biologists, physicists, computer scientists, philosophers) defines it." Nationally famous institutes, academies, and research organizations, besides professors and scholars from three or four universities of USA, were listed as participants. Hard to believe, this unknown me was cordially invited to be a speaker too! It might have been that I was being hauled up before the jury to stand trial for the impudence of having written that article, but really it was a genuine gesture that I found delightful and purposeful.

The conference is over. The result seems to be the conclusion by a powerful majority that "we do not understand what consciousness is. Discussion must continue for as long as necessary." About myself, I feel that my paper pleased the audience, was enthusiastically accepted by the non-technical and non-specialist listeners, and was indulgently smiled upon by the heavy-weights. I was told that a senior math-science professor had said, "Mr. Reddy's speech was poetic, literary, artistic and witty. I enjoyed it. But it wasn't really science." That fairly sums up the situation. I say this without rancour or resentment. In fact, I can see their view-point. And also why they need time to see the other view-point.

But it troubles me in the name of humanity to see the great barrier, like the Great Wall of China, that divides the perception of reality into two irreconcilable halves. On one side is science which declares that consciousness is an output of the brain, a product of cellular and chemical configurations, and on the other side is spirituality which maintains that the brain is only the material equipment through which the energy of consciousness manifests, and energy is not created or destroyed by equipments. In the words of the sages:

LOOK AT THE MIND AS A FUNCTION OF MATTER, AND YOU HAVE SCIENCE.

LOOK AT MATTER AS THE PRODUCT OF THE MIND, AND YOU HAVE RELIGION.

Therefore I am attempting through this treatise to set forth the outlines encompassing the "observer" of physics and the "experiencer" of neurology, to see how "consciousness" figures in these two streams of investigation. You and I need to know the answers, for where but in you and me is the voice of consciousness that raises the questions?

# 1
# WHERE IS THE BEGINNING?

Over the centuries, keen clear and committed intellects have always aspired to walk through the frontiers of knowledge and peep at horizons still unseen. There is an insatiable urge to fathom origins and ends, meanings and methods, causes and effects. As understanding expands, whatever the mind has discerned one day as truth is later denied or exceeded in the progressive quest, and honesty demands that the mind shall concede a relative falsity to its precedent assertions.

Such seekers of higher knowledge are of two distinguishable categories; scientists and philosophers.

Science encompasses the entire gamut of matter. Matter is seen in both the passive and dynamic modes, so there can be no study of matter that does not include intimately the study of energy and force. Time, Space, and Causation become vital factors. This brings in measurement, calibration, and equating. Thus Science becomes Chemistry when dealing with substances and their interactions,

Physics when dealing with interactions of matter and energy and the laws governing them, and Mathematics when dealing with the measurement of quantities and changes, and expressing them through precise equations.

However subtly the scientific investigation reaches into the dark alleys of a distant past, and whatever it determines as the starting point for matter as we know matter, at that point too there must have been an aspect of matter, though with parameters not included yet in our definitions. So science is trying to unravel precedent events and determine the precedent cause for each event. If the question at any point is, "How did this come to be?", causation-hunting must and shall continue because in that mode, the mind must trace out the "first cause" and yet be caught in its own dilemma of what caused the first cause.

But if the question is posed as, "What is matter?" and an ultimate statement demanded, the honest answer has to be "Matter is what we cannot understand." This is not an affront to the genius of science, but only a statement of inherent limitations. It does not help to say that "matter" is that which occupies space, and "space" is that which can contain matter!

# 2

# THE KNOWER AND THE KNOWN

There is another stream of enquiry in which the same question, "What is matter?", evokes the sanction of personal experience to say, "Matter is what is perceived." Anything is validated only after perception, which is the confirmation that the "thing" exists, and thereafter arises the question, "What is that thing?". Now the question is transformed into, "What is perception?". Evidently that question must be addressed to, and answered by, the perceiver. I, who am asking the question, am myself the perceiver, and I must define perception in experiential terms. The answer cannot remain impersonal.

The shifting of the enquiry from "What is matter?" to "What is perception?" has great significance, because thereby the focus has shifted from the world of matter "outside" to the world of mentation "inside".

The scientist is, and has always been, the perceiver, but the phenomenon of perception was considered irrelevant to the mystery of the perceived. Things that are hidden in darkness are revealed to our sight when they are lit. When the investigation is of the "thing", the part played by the light is not within the frame of enquiry. But in the altered frame of reference, when perception has priority over the perceived, the intellect turns its relentless gaze from the lighted objects to the light.

Light falling on any object enshrouds it and is reflected. The reflected image, which is light in the shape of the object with its contours and colours, falls on the retina. At that point it is only light. But there it is transformed. "Light" becomes "sight". I am standing there and I see the object. The perception is not where the object is, the perception is within me. The light that is falling on my retina is also falling on the wall behind me, but there is no perception taking place there. Perception is where life is. Evidently life-plus-light is sight. Life is the capacity to sense and to respond. That is consciousness. This experience of the thing seen takes place because the illumination and the perception are both allied functions of the self-same consciousness. Consciousness, knowledge, perception – these are one word, one statement. Consciousness is the light of knowledge that illumines, and also the knower who apprehends. The whole process is within consciousness. It reveals itself as both the subject and the object. Without it, who shall talk of existence?

The stream of thoughtful reasoning which concerns itself with the triad – perceiver, perception, and the perceived – and clearly sees their integration in consciousness, is philosophy. The stream of reasoning which confines its investigations to the perceived, with the conviction that the perceived is the relevant self-sufficient frame to unravel creation, is science.

Science disagrees with the postulate of philosophy, saying: Sight and light are included in our frame of enquiry, and there is neither the need nor the possibility to enlarge it. In the ultimate analysis, matter is all there is. The so-called perceiver is an epiphenomenon, already taken care of in our study of matter.

Therein lies the vexed problem of cancellation or conciliation. At the core lies the way we understand consciousness. Analogies are useful provided vain debate does not flog them to death. We normally understand light as that which illumines an object, which is then perceived by a person. Light is different from the person. That is commonplace and unobjectionable. But consciousness has to be seen as both the light that illumines and the perceiver who knows. At this centre of I-AM, which alone has the capacity to say I-KNOW, is the validation of Existence. True, the world exists. True too that it exists only in this dimension of consciousness.

In physical terms, light and the eye (a sense organ) are matched. Light has the property of being reflected by a surface (object) and the eye has the property of receiving the reflection. We have seen that this reflection, which is still only light, becomes "sight" when "life" in the eye (of the person) unites with the light. So we said light plus life is sight.

This is true of all the sense organs through which the living body transacts with the world, receiving and responding. Matter can vibrate, and the vibrations travel through space containing any material medium. The ear is so structured that it has an eardrum that can vibrate. The vibrations of the outside source are reciprocated in the eardrum. This material phenomenon becomes "sound" only when it is heard. Life plus vibration is "sound". And life is consciousness. It manifests as hearing in the ear. (When a big tree crashes by itself in a deep lonely jungle, does it make a noise?) who answers? He who raised the question. The event is registered in consciousness.

It is the same resolution for all sense perceptions, which are sight, audition, touch, taste, and smell. The similarity of a physical property shared by the object and the corresponding organ – eye, ear, skin, tongue, and nose in the above sequence – leads to paired responses. They are five different parameters, but in the person they are united in one focal point. That focus is that there is conscious recognition, or feel, or experience of whatever is sensed. In real terms it is the "knowing": I know what I see, I know what I hear, touch, taste or smell. And "knowing" is the moded consciousness.

It therefore follows that just as there was a primary link of a shared property, like reflection or vibration or pressure (for touch sensation), or particle dispersion (for smell), there must be a more fundamental commonality between the superficially differentiated world of matter that is known and the centre of perception where the knowing occurs. The known, the knower, and the linking energy of knowing, must all be aspects of one reality, and that reality has to be consciousness. Matter is known to consciousness. Consciousness is not known to matter. The ultimate resolution must rest in consciousness.

Science should not fault or refute such a thesis hastily. When science equates energy (E) and matter/mass (m), the ultimate resolution of the created universe rests in energy.

What prevails ultimately is what existed in the beginning. We started with the question, "Where is the beginning?" A possible answer is: In Consciousness.

# 3
# MIND AND BRAIN

The birth, play, and finale of consciousness was the area of enquiry occupied by philosophers and the subject was termed "spirituality". Consciousness was the facilitator of expression and experience of all human beings (scientists not excluded) and so it had the overtones of a personal entity or identity. We viewed a living person as the sum of a holistic integration. Flesh and blood, bone and brain became one body, one functioning organism. They contributed to the preservation of the physical person. But consciousness had a different dimension; it facilitated "knowing" and thinking; it went beyond physiological necessities into psychological domains, as an outreach of the body into the vastness beyond.

This effulgence or effluence is what we call the mind. Sensing, cognizing, remembering, willing, deciding, doing, all these refer to the mind. Without mind, a living person would be a living corpse. But that does not require any special or alien dispensation, says science. Man (or woman) is a physico-psychic complex being in whom the differentiated, but cooperating organs contribute the several functions to sustain the organism, namely respiration, digestion, circulation, excretion, and cognition. Cognition links the world outside with the body through sense perceptions, and links the body with the world outside, through response and reaction. Living is always a transactional two-way traffic, says science.

Bio-science insists that the body is self-sufficient for such a conscious existence. The brain is determined as the source and supplier of consciousness in the living being. The cell-structure of the brain and the synchronized chemistry of the body are the makers and manipulators of consciousness. So says science.

# 4

# Einstein, Hawking, And God At The Casino Of Creation

As long as causal determinism remained sacrosanct, an impersonal law held sway over matter. Newton had a long reign. Then it was time to put time in its place: A place of course has to be in space! Time was linked with, and accommodated in space as its fourth dimension, and measurement acquired a new meaning. Even then, there was no overlapping of the two streams, Physics and Biology. What came next in physics was indeed a quantum shift in understanding. Probability between conflicting truths emerged as the truest statement the physicist could make regarding the "reality" of an event. Subatomic units of matter revealed a dual aspect, appearing to be both particles and waves at the same time. Atomic events seemed to reveal "tendencies" rather than predeterminable accuracies, which meant the world of matter existed as probabilities and not as fixed laws. Einstein's theory of relativity redefined measurement, but the concept of quantum energy was saying no single measurement could lay claim to the reality of the event. An atomic event cannot be predicted with certainty; one can only speculate on the likelihood of its happening.

Einstein, we are told, was not too pleased with this intrusion. The creative authority, or law, or impulse, may also be called GOD to accommodate the usage of history and humanity. So Einstein, good man that he was, wanted to say that chance could not rightly be the author and arbiter of creation. He was only speaking as a physicist and not as an advocate of God in Heaven (or in the atom) when he said: "God does not play dice."

But, quantum mechanics had come to stay, because it agreed more precisely with experiment and made an outstanding contribution to technology. It was based on the "uncertainty principle" which established itself as a fundamental inescapable property of the world. There could not be a completely deterministic model of the universe, and future events could not be predicted with certainty. This ambiguity came into the equation because both the position and velocity of a particle could not be measured without disturbing one or both parameters by the quantum energy input essential for observation. It meant that whatever state could be observed was already a disturbed state and not the natural state.

Nature's frustrating denial of the scientist's aspiration to lock reality in an equation understandably led Stephen Hawking to expostulate, with much humour but some ire: "The evidence is that God is quite a gambler." He was saying that the unpredictability of the throw of the dice was the essence of the game that God built into the universe. There were probabilities amidst uncertainty about what would materialize when.

In this mode of enquiry and investigation, Physics is now looking at the physical world as an observed system (object) and the observing system (observer). The object can be a subatomic particle or an atomic process. The observation is aided by apparatus but finally it is a human being who is the observer. Unlike the apparatus, the learned scientist behind it is a conscious entity. "The end of this chain of processes lies always in the consciousness of the human observer," writes Capra in *The Tao of Physics*. Heisenberg is quoted as saying, "Natural Science does not simply describe and explain nature; it is part of the interplay between nature and ourselves." John Wheeler sees in this the need to replace the word "observer" by the word "participator" for greater precision in formulating the quantum theory. Can human consciousness be excluded in a description of the world?

5

# Is The Observer Of Physics Conscious?

The response of science to that could be: "Why are you even asking that question? Who is denying that the scientist who is enquiring into the phenomenon, and then describing it, is human and conscious?"

But that response would be sadly missing the point. The question asked is: "Is it not consciousness as an independent and separate agency, that affirms the existence of matter?" Science which insists irrevocably that consciousness is a neural output, or an oozing from the brain (perhaps akin to sweat oozing from the skin?), is stating that in the final analysis what is referred to as "mind" is also matter, for whatever is an output of matter must be modified matter, but not other than matter. Then the probe of consciousness into the reality of matter would be a farcical situation, much like the policeman who is investigating a theft, who is seen on scrutiny to be the thief himself camouflaged as a cop!

To change the metaphor, we have the painting on a canvas of a landscape with grasslands, a stream, ducks and trees, and the picture of the painter himself sitting to one side with his easel on which he is painting the scene. It is all one picture, one frame. It is a painting with the painter also pictured as painting the picture. What we are asking is: "Who is the painter of this picture?" Would it be a sufficient reply to point out that portion of the canvas which contains the picture of the painter?

The realization must dawn that the canvas cannot contain the real painter. He cannot, just cannot, be in that frame. A reflection cannot contain the subject that is reflected however perfect the likeness may seem. In fact, on contemplation, any reflection is not only unreal but also incorrect because of lateral inversion (if right is left, then whatever is left cannot be right!).

The physicists' "observer" is not a reference to the human. It (not "he") is only another temporal-spatial configuration in a larger scene that is the field of observation, yet it is assigned a special initiative. Is it a first amongst equals? The scientific surmise of the riddle seems to be that mind is comparable to a pre-programmed computer with creative capacities. But the question returns: "Who, if anyone, programmed the computer?" Capra, the renowned physicist of intellect and intuition, and author of *The Tao of Physics*, seems to be guardedly hedging his insights when he writes:

"The contrast between the two kinds of description – classical terms for the experimental arrangement and probability functions for the observed objects – leads to deep metaphysical problems *which have not yet been resolved*. In practice, however, these problems are circumvented by describing the observing system in operational terms, that is, in terms of instructions which permit scientists to set up and carry out their experiments. In this way, the measuring devices and the scientists are effectively joined into one complex system which has no distinct, well defined parts, and the experimental apparatus does not have to be described as an isolated physical entity."[1]

---

1 *FONTANA/COLLINS, 1977 edition, page 138*

I respectfully submit that the problems were resolved elsewhere, long before science saw them as problems. Metaphysics is the theoretical philosophy of "existence" and "knowledge." These are two simple words of common usage in daily life, but in the metaphysical frame, they are words of deep, fundamental and primordial significance. Anything exists and is known to exist. *There has to be existence of knowledge irretrievably coupled with the knowledge of existence.* These parameters define consciousness. Consciousness cannot be mixed up with any devices or apparatus, which are material contraptions with mechanical functions. They are insentient whereas consciousness is synonymous with sentiency.

How then can consciousness be a product of braincells which are molecules of matter, of a certain configuration, even as bone, blood, and muscle are variations of matter with other configurations? How can insentient matter give rise to sentiency? Or, is the distinction irrelevant? We, all of us, always, talk of consciousness, not as an objective perception, but as a subjective experience. Consciousness is experienced as knowing, feeling, loving, hating, remembering.

# 6

# WHAT IS CONSCIOUSNESS?

It is here that new physics may be seen as treading on the toes of bio-chemistry, but in truth there is no such discord within the scientific fraternity. Consciousness is not a word in the vocabulary of the physicist. We have had to labour for clarification only because we observed an "observer" in their description of reality. He turned out to be unreal!

It may seem now that we meandered needlessly across the meadows of physics searching for consciousness. Finding it a misguided venture, we have crossed over to the adjacent territory which flies the flag of chemistry. We said consciousness in not in the lexicon of physics, only time-space is. We must add now that time-space is not in the lexicon of chemistry; consciousness is, and very much so in bio-chemistry. But there is a rider.

If consciousness was only about feeling, about pain, emotion, or muscular response, physics could disclaim any involvement with it, but as TIME (unlike matter) is a concept and as concepts are the exclusive domain of consciousness, and physics has a vital involvement with time, we have to suspect that physics cannot distance itself from this enquiry too long. Time will catch up! Physics and chemistry may then turn out to be one seamless science. Time is an interval between two events. An event is what is cognized. Cognition occurs in consciousness. Therein lies the overlap, if not the unification, of physics and chemistry. However, that shall wait a little. Now the scrutiny is of brain and consciousness.

The great divide between science and spirituality is not whether the emphasis is on fact or faith, not the difference between experimental verification and emotional acceptance, not the provable reality of a lifespan versus the scorned and the seemingly unsubstantiated projections of life-after-death. These questions and their answers will fall into one rationale of sequential thought, if the basic frame is on solid foundations. Otherwise, as is the case now and has been for too long, the grandest abodes of human intelligence will be spacious multistorey dwellings in mansions built without a ground floor!

The foundation has to be the answer to the question:

IS CONSCIOUSNESS A PRODUCT OF THE BRAIN, OR IS CONSCIOUSNESS AN ENERGY WHICH MANIFESTS THROUGH A MATCHED EQUIPMENT WE CALL THE BRAIN??

What are we referring to when, talking together, discussing together, we use the word "consciousness"? If in conversation we use words such as iron, water, heat, world, or hunger, there is no ambiguity or vagueness in communication. Similarly, there ought to be no ambiguity about a reference to consciousness. When the other words were heard, there arose in us knowledge of the things for which those words were the assigned names. The sound of the name brought up the knowledge of the thing. This knowledge-capability is consciousness, is it not? All other learning about the world deals with acquiring the knowledge of things of the world, but this learning about consciousness centres on acquiring the knowledge of knowledge. It is a departure from the habituated occupation of our lives, but it cannot be remote or nebulous. On the contrary, it may be too close, too intimate, for the mental gaze to focus on it all of a sudden. In a day of normal activity our eyesight rests on a thousand things and serves our purposes. It is the eye that makes it possible, but in a lifetime I may not have given direct attention to the eye as the first principle and facilitator of my perpetual need to see and act and fulfil myself. Similarly, knowing and utilizing the known has been the method and definition of our living, and our preoccupation with it was self-sufficient, but now, in a spirit of deeper discovery and higher purpose, we are turning our attention from the seen to the seer, from the known to the knower. And that is why this question has framed itself: WHAT IS CONSCIOUSNESS?

Dropping the labels of scientist or philosopher, let us relate the word "consciousness" to the familiar undeniable FEEL of it in ourselves. Let us not make it an impersonal word in an encyclopaedia or get stalled in vain dialectic. It is, is it not, that inwardly revealing faculty or facility by which we, in ourselves, recognize our livingness, our perceptions and responses, our feelings and memory-recall and desire-projection? To be alive, and alive to being alive, is the insignia of "consciousness."

✦

# 7
# ENERGY IS FOR EVER

Consciousness manifests the energy that propels thoughts into constant flow. Memory, intelligence, will, desire and emotion – are all facets of the mind, and mind is a movement, a procession of thoughts. The energy comes from consciousness. Energy is the capacity for doing work and where there is movement, work is being done. Any unmanifest energy does not reveal itself. In the potential state, conscious energy exists but is not experienced; but in its kinetic form its presence is proved by the resultant movement in the thought process.

Gravity or electricity or radiation are energies that we are familiar with. They are objectively deduced, defined and measured by observing their manifested effects. Cause is never seen as cause, it is always seen in the effect it produces. These energies – we can agree on this without argument – do not "know" themselves. We call them inert or insentient. They do not know us (no loss on either side), but we know them (good for us).

We also know the energy of consciousness. But wait a minute.

Say that again. Who knows it, who is the "we" here? By our own definition, the knower is consciousness. So consciousness knows consciousness? Here, words of habitual usage are breaking down. Why? Because the words are the vehicles of relativity, born of duality and serving to demarcate opposites. Their validity is confined to a subject-object relationship. The scientist studies matter and energy which are the objects of his exploration, in relation to which he is the subject. But now he is focussing on subjectivity and there is no object, unless we say that the one is both subject and object, which makes a travesty of normal speech. There arises thus a need to make meanings more flexible, more fluid and more versatile. It cannot be otherwise on the horizon where land touches the sky, and the temporal bows to the eternal, and the relative whispers to the Absolute. To him who would investigate the ultimate reality, the unified field, or the Theory of Everything, the role of consciousness must stand out, distinct, paramount, and pristine, being a category apart. It is not the felt thing, it is the feeler; it is not the known thing, it is the knower; it is not the observed, it is the observer. If the talk turns to an amalgam of the subject and the object, the word that survives cannot be objectivity. The Subject must be king. But can there be a king without a kingdom?

It is in this context, now hopefully stated in clear and complete terms, that we return to the question: IS CONSCIOUSNESS A PRODUCT OF THE BRAIN? We shall not get distracted by devious and divisive digressions. Our enquiry into fundamentals is too sacred for that. We will anticipate and dispose of one possible impediment. Some one will rise up and ask, "At what point of biological evolution do we talk of consciousness?" We have equated consciousness with the self-recognition of life. Such recognition cannot be there in a pebble or a boulder, in a diamond, or a corpse. It must be there in an ant, an elephant, an infant and in me. All these respond to outward stimuli, and that is life, and the response is due to the conscious feel of the stimulation. So, all forms of life, insects to angels if you wish, possess the *feel* of consciousness, though the expression of it will vary depending upon the way the equipment, which is the body of the creature, is structured. The equipment can be broadly said to be the nervous system and the brain, or the equivalents thereof, serving to receive and transmit the energy.

When any energy manifests through equipments, the effects in quality and quantity depend on the structuring of the equipments in related terms. Electricity becomes light in a bulb, sound in a radio, motion in a fan, and heat in a resistance-coil. All these aspects are always the combined potential of electrical energy, and it has been thus eternally. When television was invented, electricity did not evolve with new TV potential. Second, electricity produces varying results of light in bulbs themselves, depending on whether the bulb is zero-watt or 100 watts, whether the glass is clear or coloured, whether the lamp is incandescent or fluorescent. That explanation can suffice now for an over-view of the biological landscape, from plants to insects to birds to animals to humans as foetuses or as adults. Someone may still say that is speculation, but where is speculation when we observe the *felt* impact in ourselves and ask if this subjective feeling can be produced by braincells? Each one of us is his own self-contained and self-sufficient laboratory, and the question should be processed and answered within these confines.

Science tends towards an argument that the refinement of instrumentation will lead to the widening of the horizons of understanding, but as the word horizon implies, it can only be embellishment upon the periphery, not enrichment at the core. If it is matter that is being investigated, objective studies are admittedly enhanced through progressive mechanical devices such as telescopes for cosmic observation and microscopes for atomic scrutiny. The data can measure the energy that works on matter, but cannot touch the question about the origin of the energy, which must be said to be eternal and indestructible. When a bulb is broken, the light in it dies, but not electricity. Bulbs need electricity to come alive with light, but before bulbs were invented or TVs or computers or dynamos, was the energy of electricity a precedent reality, or was it not? If it was, will it not remain the same reality even if all equipments cease to be?

The energies that science studies and specifies are insentient. They do not and cannot reveal their existence in the unmanifest mode. But the energy of consciousness is of a different dimension, sentiency. Its existence is synonymous with the awareness of I-AM. It is self-revealing. We may say consciousness knows itself and then it follows that it knows all else in creation. There is no other knower. And if we ignore the knowing, what remains?

So it is not the eye peering through the telescope at galaxies, or through the microscope at sub-atomic particles that can lead to ultimate answers about reality, but the "I" turned inward upon itself. Meditation, perhaps a maligned word in science, is only the scientific investigation of consciousness as the thing in itself, apart from its play and activity manifested as mind. When the eye sees its reflection in a mirror and studies it to good purpose, that is still science. When the eye is turned upon itself to see what can be seen, that is meditation. (Please do not take this literally, you will end up with a squint. And meditation will then be labelled as a squint in the otherwise healthy sight of science!) The study of the mind is psychology. The circuitry, the wiring, conductivity, resistance, protective fuses – all this is the organism science calls the brain with its nervous system. This is physiology. Consciousness being included in physiology, making it a product of the brain through neural discharge and chemical interaction, is the fatal blunder of "pure" science. Study of consciousness as LIFE in the abstract, and as LIVING in the flow of energy, has therefore acquired a classification outside the disciplines of normal science. It has become "Philosophy", the science of the origin, manifestation, and withdrawal of the energy of consciousness.

**Chemistry** seems to say: All is molecular. There is nothing called mind apart from matter. Structuring of molecules (proteins, amino acids, etc.) holds in its complex web the secret of life. We have the key. We call it DNA. The mystery of living organisms, of replication and mutation, from the simplest to the most complex, from microbe to man, will be unravelled upon this new frontier. Nature will be overtaken and exceeded by science. Your god has lost the race.

**Physics** seems to say: All is energy. There is nothing called matter (or mind) apart from energy. Quantum-field, a concept of energy, pervades the whole of space which thereby ceases to be dead and disinterested, and becomes instead vibrant and participatory. It is energy everywhere. What is seen and felt as matter is indeed the demarcation of regions of space in which the energy field is extremely intense ($E=mc2$).

**Philosophy** is saying: All is consciousness. Its energy appears as mind. *Mind creates and perceives matter. As Total Mind it creates and as individual mind it perceives.* Brain is the equipment in association with which the energy becomes particularized as the individual person. It is not different from electricity becoming the light in my room through the bulb in my room, while the energy of electricity is totally one cosmic pervasiveness. In association with an equipment, the infinite is seen as the finite. This is limitation. With reference to consciousness, particularization becomes personalization.

# 8
## Am I In Time, Or Is Time In Me?

What each one of us knows is this personalized consciousness and our questions shall henceforth refer to that, for there, and nowhere else, we have the authority for what we state.

What is our personal experience of consciousness? It is the flowing mental activity that we call the mind. A river is a flow, its content is water; its unit is, let us say, a drop of water. Mind is a flow, its content is consciousness, its unit is a THOUGHT. A flowing sequence of thoughts is the mind. My awareness of objects or feelings is the personal confirmation and assertion of my participatory presence in the world. Each perception, each cognition, is a thought. A thought is I-KNOW-THIS. A thought, any thought, can be no more. And, it can be no less. "I", the subject, is the knower. "This"(or that) is the object, the known. Linking the two is the KNOWING, knowledge capability, conscious energy. The object, the THING, exists and comes to be known. The thing's existence, needless to elaborate, is in time and space. Anything has to be somewhere (that is space) at some moment (that is time). But nothing, nothing else, can announce its existence. Only the

I-sense of the knower can do that. This I-ness too is part of the indissoluble amalgam that defines matter. There cannot be just the four-dimensional Time-Space in any reference to existence. It *has* to *be* the five-dimensional Time-Space-I. If we agree to refer to the personalized I-sense of the individualized mind as ego, it becomes Time-Space-Ego.

These are the *parameters* of mental activity, which, to repeat, is thought-flow. What is the *methodology* in the activity?

To continue with our metaphor, what is the methodology of elemental nature in the flow of rivers? The waters are returning to their source, which is the ocean. If we may relax the cold calculated language of science and indulge ourselves a little, "I left the sea and became a cloud," says the heart-beat of the river; "I became rain and soaked the land; I became a spring, a stream, a pond, a lake maybe; then cloud again and flowed again; and now finally I am a stronger current blessed with the promise of home coming; I cannot wait to merge in my source."

All things return to their source. So does the mind of man. And if it is determined rationally that mind is not matter (the way matter is matter), then mind escapes the destiny of the body cells that decay and disintegrate at the point of time called death. If we can postulate the status of consciousness *before* it inhabited and caused movement as a mind beyond argument, it would have the same status *after* the mental activity ceased. So *before* my birth where was the potential energy that now proclaims I-am-so-and-so, thumping egoistically the chest of this body-mind-conglomerate? What becomes of it when this body dies?

Here we have to pause a while and re-examine our easy belief that Total Consciousness has been fragmented into individualized consciousness. We have postulated on that basis that there are as many "minds" as there are "brains", that these are separate "parcels" of consciousness each with its content of personal memories and desires, each parcel placed in its own frame of time and space. If that be so, what separates them? What is between the parcels?

That is easily answered, one may say. Space separates them (add time if you want to). The question follows: Where is space? One has to say: Space is out there, everywhere. Next question: Does Space say so? Of course not, how can it? That is the point of this enquiry, that consciousness which cognizes space is what validates the statement. Space is a thought in me, it is a content of my consciousness, not the container of it. So one would have to say that anything has to be inside consciousness, and nothing can be outside it. More correctly, *there can be no "outside" to Totality.* Then it follows that the word "inside" is meaningless, because "outside" and "inside" are related and opposed; without one the other has no relevance.

All the words of our language have arisen from our perceptions, and all the perceptions are of relativity. The words are on linear scales, and convey limitations. Whatever is measured is limited. When words have to be used for the Absolute (as distinct from the relative), the outlines of the meanings that we have by long custom and usage bestowed upon the words, must melt and mingle and gain a new sense. We have arrived at a point where it is not jargon, nor prattle, and the intellect of scientific enquiry has to ask: "Am I in time, or is time in me? Am I in space, or is space in me?" Can space be divided? Yes, we tend to say through habitual usage of words. We will say this is hall-space and beyond it is the compound-space. The four walls define the hall-space. But where are the walls standing? In space of course; but, we say, they have occupied space and demarcated it. Tell me, if we break down the walls, do we have to bring bag-fulls of space and fill up the gaps? Space cannot be denied, it cannot be fragmented. All is within space alone. Space was never conditioned, only our perception of it was.

9

# WHERE CAN SPACE GO FOR A STROLL?

Physics helps us in understanding the consistent law or laws valid for the whole material universe, though physicists may not have had any such generous intentions of endorsing philosophy. Physics tells us that matter in a void called space has come to be viewed as a sort of high density of space itself. We have seen already that "Quantum Field", a concept of energy, pervades the whole of space, and consequently, space ceases to be dead and disinterested. Space becomes instead vibrant and participatory. Intense energy fields in space are seen and felt as matter. Energy and matter are two aspects of one reality. But science does not say there was matter and it became energy. If all is resolved into one first cause, into one ultimate word, that word would be ENERGY and not matter.

How better to denote Consciousness than to say it is self-aware space! For, like space, it is infinite. Why, even space is accommodated in it. It is the ultimate energy-field that is all-pervasive, and what we call personal mind and perceived matter are dense areas of focussed consciousness. The first cause has to be Consciousness.

Now we can see the deep import of the words of a contemporary sage who declared:

"LOOK AT THE MIND AS A  FUNCTION OF MATTER AND YOU HAVE SCIENCE. LOOK AT MATTER AS THE PRODUCT OF THE MIND AND YOU HAVE RELIGION." [Nisargadatta Maharaj, in I AM THAT.]

Let us go back to the question of what could be the state of total Consciousness that has not manifested as a thought through the equipment of a brain. It would have to be ABSOLUTE, there being nothing besides. Absolute Consciousness would be OMNISCIENT, that is, all-knowing, because "knowing" is of thoughts, and as fish can only live in water, thoughts can only swim in consciousness. It would be OMNIPRESENT, since space (and time) in which any presence resides, is itself residing in consciousness. It would be OMNIPOTENT, that is all-powerful, because, consciousness is synonymous with that supreme energy behind creation which manifests as Knowledge, Will, and Action. (*Jnana-Sakti, Iccha-Sakti, and Kriya – Sakti* are three-fold functions of *Chit–Sakti*, the power of Consciousness.)

Omniscient, Omnipresent, Omnipotent – is there one word to express this confluence? There is, but we don't want to hear it, we would rather get rid of it by saying it is not scientific. By God, we will not use the forbidden word! But as every idea needs a word, we will call it The Absolute.

So Absolute Consciousness is perforce still, that is, motionless. How can it move? Can Mr. Space take a walk? He cannot, for want of other space to move into. Absolute Consciousness is *pure being.* I postulate it, but I have no experience of that state; because, the Absolute is BEING and the relative is BECOMING. But I do have *personalized* experience of consciousness as *my* thought-flow, a movement, a process. I am part of a changing evolving entity of ego-sense. If the Absolute is like a still and silent ocean, I am like a wave upon it. As a wave I am born, I exist, I die. As a wave I have a perceived individuality and an independence. If the ocean knows itself as one massive unit, I as a wave amongst waves know it not. If my felt reality of myself as a wave is discredited as a relative reality, that is all the knowledge of myself that I possess. But how did I come to be this partite consciousness, this limited being?

I insist that there is creation and it must have had a beginning. I demand a reply. The Absolute is silent. The Absolute does not transact with the relative. So I myself postulate the reply. The Absolute static potential has to launch itself on a voyage as kinetic thought. *The motionless ocean has to create the first wave.* A wave, even the thought-wave of consciousness, must have amplitude and frequency. Amplitude denotes *space* and frequency denotes *time*. So the creative urge can only ride on conceptual space-time. That is the first kinetic urge, the first de-rating of the Absolute, the first compromise of perfection, the first disturbance in still and silent consciousness. On this frontier that we call the beginning, space and time are conceptual *points*. They are dimensionless. That they become measurable staggers my understanding. It has to be the impossible made possible. It may be the slightest shiver, but consciousness-space had to *create an extension to space*. A water–wave can rise upon the surface of the sea, because the sea is limited in space. There is air–space above the water into which the sea can extend as a wave. But how can a wave rise in space itself? Consciousness is so pervasive that it cannot be moded into a thought–wave. And yet the conceptual "wave" of space–time has to arise in consciousness as the generative idea of creation. The impossible has to be rendered possible on the emerging border of the Absolute and the relative. It is *there* and *then* that time is born, but as yet what is born is the *concept* and not the measurable. In the conceptual frame the precise words would be here and now. Intellectually we can understand that here would condense to a dot in space and now would shrink to an instant in time; whereas there is a distance away and then is a time-span removed. On this reckoning, here and now would be a tentative blemish as an adjunct to the Absolute, but there and then would be an outright denial of the Absolute, measurable extentions to dimensionless infinity, a broken logic. Remember the ancestor who fell from paradise? This is it, giving credence to relativity. This is it, the original sin.

This is the beginning of a self-imposed limitation of a personal identity in *time* and *space*, followed by the natural corollary of otherness (plurality), followed by a desire for relating one with the other.

In our perceived projection and speculation, which is the understanding of the relative (the created), what an explosion it must have been that altered the precedent state of the Absolute (the creator)! Though no more than the smallest SMALL SHAKE in Absolute Consciousness, it has to be visualized as comparatively more potent, more powerful, more awesome and majestic than any BIG BANG of choked and throttled mass of gasping matter.

My mind cannot know space-time as points. To me *space* and *time* have perforce to have dimensions. I experience them as intervals, not as stationary points. Between two objects is my measured *space*. Between two events is my measured time. I am the cognizer. *All that is cognized is relative.* Time-space integration into creation has ensured that. There can only be a Theory of Relativity, there cannot be a Theory of the Absolute. Of course relativity can talk, define, distort or deny the Absolute, but that too would be in relative terms. *The name of mind is Relativity.*

In the Absolute frame, existence and knowledge are not two words, they are one. Absolute Consciousness may be said to be existence of knowledge, and equally correctly, knowledge of existence. But partite consciousness, which is I-am-this-person ego-sense, exists through knowing, that is, thorough knowledge of existence. Descartes, the famous western philosopher, is unduly eulogized for having said: *"Cogito ergo sum"*, "I know, therefore I am." It is the right statement of relative reality, but only that. Descarte erred in concluding that *thinking* was synonymous with *being,* and that this understanding of the ego-I was the ultimate revelation. On the contrary, thinking is what leads the person (I) through the merry-go-round (sorrow-go-round?) of individual existence. Thinking means having *thought after thought,* and evidently that is the same as experiencing being *after being.* It renders "I" as a being that is constantly changing. Then, the word for it is "becoming", not "being". The distinction between the Absolute and the relative lies precisely in this, but it is no small diversity. The *thinking – I* is impossible outside the frame of time-space-causation. That "I" is compulsively propelled by the past into the future, a sequence of becomings. When "I" denotes the Absolute Totality of Consciousness, time-space-causation are irrelevant and impossible. Einstein's equation of mass and energy, and Descartes' equation of subjectivity and objectivity, are both great revelations in relativity, but they do not refer to the Absolute. Einstein accepted as much when he told the scientific fraternity: "As long as the laws of mathematics refer to reality they are not certain, and as far as they are certain they do not refer to reality." Scriptures have guided us into greater transcendental awareness of Reality. The Vedas of the Hindus have said: *"Prajnanam Brahma,"* – Total Consciousness is the Absolute. Christian scriptures have said *"Jehovah"* – I am that I am. These are far greater declarations than Descartes' "Cogito ergo sum," I know, therefore I am. If they are right, Descarte is wrong, or at the least deficient in not recognizing that no statement about relativity could reveal Absolute Reality. Descarte's "I am" is the pretentions ego-sense of the person, not the "I am" of *Jehova.* Reality is not available for compromise.

This enquiry is not an academic exercise, but a vital input if I want to see my place and my purpose in creation. I can see my purpose as the quest for happiness. It is yours too, and yours. All creatures are forever seeking fullness within, a contentment, a repose. The act of seeking concedes two things: One, what is sought by me is known to me; two, it is missing in me now. Happiness may be a negative statement too, as avoidance of what I dislike, or elimination of pain or sickness. All these desires, which are goals, require interaction with the world, require relating which is a web of cause and consequence. I have convinced myself that desires can be ended through success and satiation, but this psycho-physical ME finds that the shopping list of desires keeps changing but never gets exhausted. My body-identification sees the inevitability of aging and dying, and time threatens and terrorizes me.

What is this time? Is it not strange that we mentally accept the passage of time? *Time* passes. But we don't say that about space. *We* pass through *space*, while *space* stays put. Yet our physics has handcuffed *space* and *time* together. One would expect that both move or both stop. Scientists and psychologists must sort out this paradox.

What is this *time*? Let me ask: What is the river? As I watch the river, the water is constantly changing. The water this second is not the material of the preceding second or of the following one. Yet I perceive a constant identity I call the river and the identity runs through the changing content of its substance. That identity is created by the linking in my mind of the thousand sequential visuals my eyes have perceived. Without memory I could not experience the river. Now let us look at my mind, my river of flowing thoughts. Since (as stated earlier) I, (meaning this ego-person mode of consciousness), is rising and falling sequential with each thought-wave of "I-know-this," I must be a *recurrence* generated afresh with each thought, but I need to feel I am an *unbroken occurrence*. My existence cannot be a series of disconnected dots, it must be a continuous line. I retain a continuing identity of myself and I am lost without it. I am not me without it. So what shall I do? I need a string on which the beads can be strung to hold as a "*mala*", a rosary. This is vital. Therefore the creative impulse or intelligence of the Absolute that played at a relative modification of itself, whereby you and I emerged as the created beings with spatial and temporal limitations, gave us time as the string. TIME IS THE THREAD ON WHICH ARE STRUNG PERCEPTIONS TO MAKE UP MEMORY. What can I be without memory? So *time* has been created to serve my needs, but I have ignorantly bestowed a sovereignty on *time* and surrendered before it as its slave. The imposter, *time*, has grabbed the opportunity by holding out the threat of DEATH. The movement is mine, for the energy for movement belongs to consciousness. I loaned my energy to *time* as a master gives a loan to his servant, but I suffered ignorance of my true state and forgot who was the lender and who the borrower. My ignorance and its exploitation by *time* have made me pledge my life to *time*. What a mockery!

# 10
## DARWINISM: UNPAID WAGES AND UNEARNED INCOME

"Split personality" is a problem the psychologist deals with. It concerns the individual. Split INTO personality is the problem the sage addresses. It concerns cosmic creation. The basic problem to be resolved is how Total Consciousness, indivisible and indestructible, is being sensed and experienced by each one of us as partite mentation, individualized, embodied, and therefore subject to decay and death. How could the split take place?

That is the position I am in as a person. If the Absolute which is infinite has become a finite number, that number will fulfil itself when it returns to infinity. If the number believes in its ignorance that addition will one day make it infinity, it has to try it out till it realizes that the largest list of the largest numbers will not add up to infinity. Only then will the methodology be corrected. Our game of desire satiation is the same, but we are still saying, "Give me a chance to add more numbers." While doing so the person dies.

The body, which was always a corpse, an insentient conglomerate of matter, is empowered by the energy of consciousness, which inhabits the dwelling. The dwelling thereby gains a semblance of sentiency, and we say he is alive. When the occupier takes brief periodical holidays there is the deep-sleep-state, but when he abandons the dwelling altogether, the house disintegrates and collapses. We say he died. Wrong, sir. We may say the house died.

But what happened to that energy, or the inner person? We will come to that. At this juncture we first need to take a look at Darwin. By his dedicated collection and codification of data, partly visible and mostly buried, he put together the temporal sequence of living forms. He chronicled the structural changes in construction and mobility of bodies to survive in changing and often hostile environments. The changes were in the building blocks of the living creature, and therefore the progeny resulting from the transfer or transmission of bodily cells naturally started off with that advantage of enhanced capital. *Lucky son, it was his unearned income.* He quietly inherited the benefits of the sustained labours of generations past. The father died, his labours terminated, unceremoniously. Whatever harmony he had established with his environment, and whatever supremacy he had earned in the battle for survival, there was no provision for restful retirement. *Unlucky fellow, his was a case of unpaid wages.* Over a period of time, as generation followed generation, was there a link in terms of continuity of experience? Was there a purpose sustained and furthered?

"What 'purpose' in creation?" is the rebuke and retort of science. "Natural laws go on and on, producing results. An eternity of Time offers an infinity of probabilities. Change is a game of chance, not of intentions. *Science studies the changes and reconstructs the sequences to understand the working of energies in nature.* If you talk of purpose, you are postulating a presiding mind where such purpose is conceived, lodged and programmed. Whose mind? You introduce a creator and call that GOD. It is not rational. It is not scientific."

If the arithmetic of progressive numbers can seal off one end with an infinity and the other end with a zero, even though the linear progression cannot touch either concept, and if that is perfectly scientific, the scientist needs to take a closer and calmer look at the Absolute and the relative. Those whom human history calls the sages have always done that. In fact that is all they needed to do, for two sound reasons: First, the scientists and the rationalists were doing a good job of understanding the complexities of "relative reality"; second, as the higher naturally holds the lower within its orbit, the Absolute includes within itself all that can be known about relativity. No number knows infinity, but infinity knows them all! The awakened mind of man cannot but be overwhelmed by the magnificence and majesty, immensity and intricacy, vibrancy and variety in creation.

Along with that there is interdependence and harmony, the utility of each in the perfection of the whole. *There is an amazing replication of design common to the atom and the universe, as though spherical geometry and circular motion had to be the choiceless basics of the architect.*

It is the intelligence in a created being that observes, enjoys, and applauds this cosmic splendour of which the earth and the planets, in their ceaseless drift through space, know nothing (and careless). And yet science eschews "Intelligence" as the source and sustenance of the method and momentum behind creation, disowns "Ideation" or "will" as being words of no relevance, and bestows the honour and sovereignty upon Time and Chance!

If the scientist, whose intellect and honesty of conviction are not called into question, says so, let it be. Refusal to accept conclusions till observation and repeatable experimentation establish their validity, is the hall mark of a scientist. But disagreement does not give either discipline the licence to denigrate the other. As Shakespeare's Antony says, standing over the stabbed body of Julius Caesar,

"But Brutus says he was ambitious,

And Brutus is an honourable man,"

so let me intone "Science says philosophy has over-reached, and science is an honourable judge."

The fault, as generally happens, is shared by both. The philosopher often sits on his fancied peak and will not reach out a hand of understanding across the rugged foothills of relativity which his young scientist friend has explored so vigorously. The need is to include first and then exceed. Nothing is or can be faulted, because the revelations of science are not faulty. They are *limited*. "What is wrong with the limitation of knowledge?" fumes the scientist. "The horizons are forever expanding, are they not?"

What is wrong is this, that you are saying one of two things:

1) That the relative will one day take us to the Absolute, which is the same as saying the limited will take us to the limitless. Sir, it means we are erring in our grasp of the *limits of limitation*. To stand corrected there would be the first prerequisite for transcendence.

2) Or, you are saying that there is not, and cannot be, a leap into Absolutism as it is only a myth of relativity. If you say so, then please be consistent and do not talk of final answers about creation and time. Do not refer to "Reality" because, given the ultimate reach of its meaning, Reality or Truth is that which never gets sublated or superceded, is constant, true, and beyond falsification in the three periods of time, the past, the present, the future; that is to say, unconditioned by time and space and causation. How can a theory of relativity aspire to frame Reality?

Then, one may say, talk of Absolute Reality or the Truth-of-Everything should be taboo to scientist and sage alike. If mind is the common tool of relativity, how can it serve the sage selectively to go beyond? The sage too uses his mind, which, as with the scientist, is a tool of relativity. How can the sage reach and teach Absolutism, when the same attainment is denied to the scientific quest? What does the sage convey when he refers to Reality or God? (Good question.)

The sages themselves were only student philosophers acquiring knowledge while they were researching and reaching out for the meaning of Reality. They became sages only when they experienced Reality. Knowledge of things is objective. What is known is separate from the Knower, who is the subject knowing the object. Subjective knowledge can only be knowledge of oneself – we may say, one's self.

There the word 'knowledge' becomes irrelevant and improper; the word 'experience' is more appropriate. The self is the reality of consciousness, the only Reality. The transcendence is from knowing to Being. Whoever has made the transition is a sage. A parable is useful to illustrate the point. Please permit me.

A salt-doll decided to measure the depth of the ocean. It had a feeling of affinity, a vague sense of shared identity with the sea and wanted to investigate. As soon as it dived into the water, it melted. Now who could tell how vast or deep the ocean was? Not that the salt-doll had failed in its mission, it did gain the total experience. There was total identification with the saltiness of the ocean, the fluidity, the depth and vastness, its deep repose and external turbulence, its shelter to a world of creatures, its majesty and power. There was no duality any longer of salt-doll and salty ocean, no relating, there was only the seemless fusion into oneness. The petty, temporal, unreal individuality of a doll had been transcended. I-the-salt-doll had transmuted itself into I-the-ocean.

Understood, you say. Beautiful story, you say. And rightly ask: Tell me, who is to come back and tell us of the ocean now?

I am glad you are asking the question, says the sage with a happy smile. It shows you are listening. Previously your colleagues were running away offended as soon as I said "Let me tell a story." They seemed to say: "What else have you done all your life but tell stories?"

# 11
## AN ETERNITY OF TIME,
## OR TIMELESS ETERNITY?

Now for the answer:

Physics is the study of matter and the energies that act on matter. Meaning no insult to either, let us describe them as dead matter and dead energies.

Physics turns to bio-science and politely enquires: "You study living organisms. What is the basic departure?"

Bio-science says: "To be honest, our study too is centred in the same material. The life we study is a product of dead matter too (if you want to call it that). When carbon, nitrogen, hydrogen, oxygen, calcium et al combine in certain configurations, the resultant molecules called proteins or aminoacids et al, become the originators of what we call life."

Whatever is a product of matter must be material too. Are we to understand that "life" is only a word that refers to a "dead" phenomenon? And that as gravity stands in relation to matter, even so does consciousness stand in relation to brain? That death is the true face of creation, and life a mask laid falsely upon it?

The whole argument would end there, peacefully and decisively, if consciousness is in truth an effervescence of the brain, that is to say it is only refined matter. Then mind would be subject to all the limitations of matter in relativity. But such is not the case. Gravity has no awareness when it relates to matter, there is no subject-object differential. But when consciousness relates to a thing, the thing is an object of awareness, and there is a positioning of consciousness as the subject. This sets consciousness apart, the only one of its category, beyond comparison with other energies in creation. By this uniqueness it is poised to share the uniqueness of Absolutism. It has the licence and can make the entry. The entry is denied to anything that is limited by the conditioning of time and space.

I-ness, I-am-ness, I-know – they all refer to one focal point of my existence, they are indicators of one basic impulse of life in me. And that is Self-Awareness. This is the licence I have, which the inert world of matter has not.

I possess this I-centre. I have circumscribed it with the life I have lived as this person and have called it my mind. The circle encloses the memories, desires and hopes of the person that is *me*. The circumference is the limit of my individuality, and the content is the history of events and responses relating to this body, which is this person, which is me.

I exist and I accumulate a memory. The memory is not indispensable for my existence. It can be annulled, the history can be totally wiped out, but that would only mean that the circumference is erased. The centre remains intact, because the I-ness exists. That is not lost or changed. But what is it the centre of? When the limitation has gone, there is the unlimited. Therefore the centre without a measured circle drawn around it is the centre of immeasurable space itself. The I-ness of unlimited unitary consciousness was reduced to an ego-sense of individual personality because of the identification with a physical frame. It then suffered the delusion of being the body (from toe-nail to brain) with a brief existence in time and space subject to birth and death. Redeemed from the error, I-ness is seen as a centre without a circumference. Then, anywhere is the centre of everywhere. The linearity of a diameter is over, the opposite ends of relativity have been united to forge a circle, and the area of a circle has become a point (of nil area). Yet this point itself is also the whole expanse. This I-AM-ness is all of consciousness. The relative has yielded the rightful place to the Absolute.

"I-am" is the experiencing centre, the awareness. Therefore the "I" that started the quest, finally arrives at the experience of the Absolute. There is no loss, there is only an incomparable gain. *The salt-doll has not lost itself, it has gained the ocean.* It can never again suffer the delusion of limitation. It can clear the doubts of all salt-dolls, and tell them of their true potential, their origin and abode.

But listening to the Guru of self-realization can only promote verbal understanding in the student. The luminosity of the Guru can add lustre to the student's intellect, the love can enhance the receptivity, but ultimately, the experience must be gained by oneself for oneself.

## 12

# SHALL WE REFLECT ON LIGHT?

"The luminosity of the Guru can add lustre to the student's intellect," we have just said and almost inadvertently we have touched an important aspect of scientific study and speculation, LIGHT; for the words "luminosity" and "lustre" refer to light which is a significant – even dominating – aspect of our perceived reality, the domain of science.

It happens that LIGHT is also a weighty (while weightless) word of philosophy. Long before Einstein reportedly declared "for the rest of my life I want to reflect on what light is," another stream of enquiry or wisdom had declared "God said 'Let there be light'". (If science asks whether God was seated, or more guardedly asks situated, (for He could have been standing) in darkness before there was light, the question topples over itself by musing, "Was there darkness before there was light? If so, how did darkness come to be?") This must imply that "God" denotes a prior existence and light comes later. The word "later" has brought in time (when time comes, shall space be far behind!) and a creative pulse.

It has also been declared that God is the light of heaven and of the earth; the words God and light get equated, and God would then be, to say the least, the first factor of created reality, sense-recognized as light only, but missed as godliness due to some persistent ignorance cast as a veil. In this context ignorance would equate to darkness, and again the question arises "whence this darkness." If in our language – that is to say, with the habituated words that we, scientists spiritualists and laymen alike, are stuck with – we have to make sense of Reality, first we have to isolate "Being" and "becoming" and then link them into creator-creation. So we postulate a beginning, the undefinable Lordship of Absolute Being; and in that we infer an impulse to launch itself on a trillineum trip. "I must have time and space for the trip" It muses, "but I do not have conceptual space into which I can pack them. So I must create through conceptualization space-of-consciousness (chid-akasa). How will I bring about this illusory plurality?" He laughs silently to Himself. "I am pure light. Let there be reflected light, which will be me only, but as reflected consciousness. Thus there will be illumination along with time and space. Space will contain my many images as created things, time will facilitate their movement and interactions as becomings, and reflected consciousness as mind will provide the light of knowledge. It will all be me and nothing but me – how else? – but my Truth will be concealed and not self-evident. Neither accepted altogether nor denied altogether, I will watch from my hide-out within their own minds, as scientists and spiritualists argue endlessly!

If science will tolerate an undefinable "intuition" as the basis of a pronouncement, St. John has said that the soul is a perfect image of God. The word "image" has brought in a new dimension to the discussion; we are now talking of reflections. Einstein, I venture to say, did not have this in mind when he exulted "For the rest of my life I want to reflect on what light is." If he had focussed on reflected light he might have seen in the makings of the mind subtler intricacies than he saw in the makings of matter. He delved into the depths of relativity convinced that on its ocean-bed he would grab the immersed crest-jewel of Absolutism. But that can never be. The ocean does not hold the sun, only on its surface is a teasing play of tossed reflections.

So too unmanifest consciousness is the sun knowledge and the cosmos a play of its emitted light that becomes our perceived knowledge. The world is an image. Image of one self-same Reality (some call it God). True your face is different from mine but that is because mind-mirror is by design an uneven surface, and a billion variations in images arise out of a billion possibilities of distortion. But scientist or philosopher, our residential address in creation is the same: BEHIND THE MIRROR.

The total frame of cosmic enquiry must include matter and mind, cosmic energies and operational consciousness, time, space, mass, and light, till relativity is robbed of its relation and the Absolute is restored to its beyond. BEYOND? Beyond time, beyond space, beyond cosmic constants? Yes, beyond all those. Yet this has to be done by the mind, through concepts turned to symbols turned to words (sounds); for mind is its thoughts; thoughts are their own things; and things have their names (words). All our words are sound-structures, shaped and assembled for remembrance, recognition, recall and communication. They are born out of, and shaped, by all that lived and lives, and all the experiences. But all experiences always have been in the relativistic frame (and sufficient thereto) and limited. If the mind reaches out and beyond to something (a 'thing' again?) that is not an extension of relativity, but (call it) a transcendence for which the mind has shaped and secured its word-symbol "Absolutism", what is it trying to do, and how does it aspire to achieve the goal? Of what use are words here, and without words, of what use is mind for the task?

Therefore it becomes imperative at this juncture of search or research to pause, to find a perch on silence and take an unhurried look at WORDS, so that we may concede their full potential, while also marking their limitations.

The history of man and his mind is a tale of relating amongst many, for profit, pleasure or information. Call it sensing, feeling, or knowing, the event is categorized and can be measured. All measurement is on a linear scale – small and large, short and tall, heat and cold, poor and rich, ugly and beautiful, sentient and insentient. In this dictionary of related comparable words in pairs, relativity itself could not bear to stand companionless, and so matched or contrasted itself with "absolute", a pairing achieved by a negation of its own soul, dragging the beyond into the here. The result is only a travesty of words and meanings.

And yet the soaring intellect searching for ultimates must find here a sufficiency of method and material to reach its irresistable goal. This, thank God – sorry, that word God is again a travesty, so thanks wherever thanks are due – is possible, because words have a hidden dimension and unsuspected momentum. On the linear scale, the opposed words are perpetually interchangeable. "Hot" is one degree above "cold", but at the next degree that "hot" has become "cold". Same with short and tall, dark and fair, poor and rich, words are not deterministic, they are probabilistic. By habit of common useage, words have become to our minds caged birds with clipped wings. When the rare intellect releases them upon the pastures of virgin contemplation, the cramped wings are stretched, the stiffened legs regain their hop, the silenced voice recollects its song, and joy sparkles in the eyes. The forgotten flutter returns, and the bird is on the wing. Buoyed by success and propelled by instinct, the word that is the bird frolicks in loops and dives, and intoxicated with joy and hope soars in dizzying circles of ascent and rises upon a spiral higher and ever higher. Leave the birds awhile to their hour of delight. We will join them later. Right now we have to pick up another thread that runs through the warp and weft of the fabric we are weaving.

# 13
# IMAGES AND ILLUSIONS

Return to the enquiring mind. In its inescapable frame of relativity, all values are recognized in duality, set in opposition, and seen as positive to one side of any location and negative to the other side. The material scientist has to answer to himself, some day in the progression of his quest, which of the opposing words will endure. ENDURE should mean, last out in time. If time comes (or goes?) to a halt, the question is itself invalidated, for what is to endure if time does not? Seen in the frame of time, the negatives endure. The sun will burn out and there will be no light, no heat, indeed no life. Darkness, cold and death will prevail. No work or movement is conceivable. Entropy swallows energy.

What about MIND? someone asks. The bio-scientist looks at the physicist and hesitantly nods in mute assent. He pontificates: "Mind is a play in consciousness. Consciousness is a play of neural responses to molecular interactions in the brain. Finally mind lies buried in the debris of matter. This is the void, the finale, the reign of Negativity. For how long? That question should be asked of Time, but Time died before you could ask. What then? SILENCE.

Silence which is the voice of Death. So much for your god, your ultimate Reality."

Perfectly "scientific", rational and logical, if – a crucial IF this – consciousness were a product of brain-cells (matter). That has to be examined *ad nauseum*, without offending scientific discipline.

Suppose consciousness is X, the unknown factor.

**Immediate objection:** "But consciousness is in my knowing. I speak of it from experience, so it is the known."

**Answer:** Suppose further that the personalized consciousness that you speak of (I would, too) is not the Thing-in-itself but a transacted presence of it, that therefore the same word would refer to X in parameters totally distinct, and different. In that case we need to use available words dexterously to distinguish what is same from what is similar. The need arises to talk of "reflected consciousness" and "relative reality."

**Objection:** You seem to be hedging to bring in later an inadmissible god.

**Answer:** No fast-forward please. Any case, I will not be provoked. We are trying to write an equation, in which X has not yet been resolved. Your knowing, functional, and particularized consciousness, will now be seen as an integral part of your relative frame, because "knowing" must admit of a knower as the subjective aspect and the known as the objective part, linked by the potential "knowability" (or the inherent potential to know). The relationship of knower and known makes it an integral aspect of relativity. Descarte's *"cogito, ergo sum"* belongs here – "I know, therefore I am" – with emphasis on "therefore." One may add, "without knowing I am not". (Latinize it, if you wish – and can.) Without knowing, the thing that was to be known, is also not. Then, what is the Thing-in-itself that you are searching for?

*It cannot be found in relativity. It cannot be missed in the Absolute.*

**Question:** What is X in all this?

**Answer:** It has to be the Absolute. Absolute Consciousness, the Reality that seems to have become the reflected reality of the cosmos, the Creator-Thing that produced the images of cosmic things out of nothing, the Positive that pretended the negative can exist by itself (in negative existence).

**Question:** How and where could the Absolute reflect and project an image?

**Answer:** When? How? And why? are persistent questions of mentation. In totality, they are addressed to creation. Answering them is understandably the scientists' passion. Philosophy, with seers as the accredited spokesmen, has offered answers. At the apex, if the scientist may be read as saying "matter does not contain matter ", why not transcendence be heard as proclaiming. " There is no creation apart from Absolute Consciousness. It – this C – is pure being. There never was a becoming – till you came along, and swore by time, and space, and cause-effect cascade of becomings.

**Question:** I must interrupt. This world of time, space, and causality is constantly experienced by me. I am conscious of it. You say this is a reflected reality.

**Answer:** Exactly. Because you insist and demand an answer for an invalid question, a tentative answer has to be given and the discussion carried forward. Only then there is ground to proceed to solve X, we cannot give up, we need to proceed together.

You have made your consciousness the proof of your world. Your knowing it confirms its existence to you. Where was your world in your state of deep sleep, a state of nescience totally free of thoughts? Nothing (no thing) "exists" that is not "known" to exist. You, who knew your world in your waking-state, did not yourself exist to yourself in your deep-sleep state. You were unaware, totally unaware. You were not there as reflected consciousness. But you had not perished. Your ego-sense, the I-am-this-person-sense, had vanished, but evidently not perished, because you woke up (welcome) and resumed your identity as the same person. You had a continuing existence and identity, you had remained intact but latent as the Thing, the Reality, the X, Therefore, and not otherwise, the reflection, the image, the relative reality, could manifest again.

**Question:** You mean if a thing is not present to the mind, it does not exist?

**Answer:** Listen to these flippant, yet profound, lines (author unknown to me):

> *There was a young man who said "God,*
> *To you it must seem very odd*
> *That a tree as a tree*
> *Simply ceases to be*
> *When there is no one about in the quad."*

> *And God replied:*
> *"Young man, your astonishment is odd,*
> *I'm always about in the quad*
> *And that is why the tree*
> *Never ceases to be*
> *As observed by yours faithfully, God."*

The point being made is that the knowledge-field of the energy of consciousness pervades all of space always, and it cannot be otherwise.

The ego in us, which is personalized consciousness imbedded

in "I-am-this-body" conviction, has no independent existence, as an image cannot be said to have an independent existence inside the mirror (the mirror has no inside). All the seeming truth of multiplicity, activity and interaction amongst images cannot be correctly assessed till one observes the subject that is reflected and relates the subject to the reflection.

**Question:** Who observes the subject and relates it to which reflection?

**Answer:** That is the fundamental question. Self-evidently this cannot be done by the reflection. The scientist standing before a mirror concedes a true replication of his nose and beard (if the beard is the insignia of his trade and rank), but he will never say that his mental activity is also taking place in the reflection's head. Form is replicated in the reflection, but not consciousness. Therefore consciousness is alone and there is nothing besides to relate to. Relating seems to arise when the images hallucinate their self-sufficient existence, and believe they possess ego-centred individualities. It would be wrong to say that images think. If you still say so, then add that whatever they think has to be wrong. (Image-inary!)

This is the enigma. This is the real "twin paradox" that science has not even suspected, being engrossed with relativity, which is an expanse of linear time and space and velocities, taking it to be the only and total vista for investigation.

The core of the teaching of all scriptures through their various "seers" or sages has focussed on this twin paradox of the seeming simultaneity, but really inseparable identity, of I-the-totality and I-the-person. The resolution of the paradox by them is complete and wholesome and final. (I draw my intimations primarily from Hindu Vedanta, and the voice most acceptable and lucid to me has been that of Ramana Maharshi.) The seers of many ages in many lands have said this in unison; for, Truth (when experienced, not speculated) can only be one. Reality cannot have a cousin. The probe is into Absolutism and relativity. The only relevant factor is consciousness. The science–for science it is–of philosophy (more loosely, or wrongly termed spirituality, religion, mysticism, or even para-psychology) resolves as convincingly as language can the dichotomy of creator and creation. But the available instruments of the probe, which are WORDS, have to be sharpened, even reshaped, and used with subtlety.

**Question:** The mirror.....

**Answer:** I am coming to that now. Thank you for having been patient, though ruffled, all this time.

It is an analogy, a reasoning from parallel cases. When space is a content of consciousness, how can we talk of locating consciousness in space? By "mirror" we must understand an inherent creative possibility (intelligence) in the Absolute, an exceeding of words and meanings till the Absolute is said to reflect itself within Itself, and create multiplicity and itself play within as so many shadows with so many shadows. The Original, the "mirror" and the "reflections" constitute one undifferentiated factor.

**Question:** Impossible. That can never be.

**Answer:** I agree. It never was. I have been saying that too all along in undertones.

**Question:** You are playing with words.

**Answer:** Rather, let us return to the play of birds that are words.

✿

# 14
# BOTH SCIENCE AND PHILOSOPHY NEED PRACTISING PRIESTS

Upon the wide pastures bathed in sunlight, with the vast expanse of blue skies above, we gaze into space for the words in their flight of freedom. We see receding specks in frenzied ascent, striving for deeper meanings and loftier purposes till an infinite potential vaguely sensed must be actualized into experience. The source of light is beckoning, the source of sound is listening, distinctions are lost, differences are reconciled. Henceforth a mere meeting will not suffice, a merger alone can be fulfilment. And so it shall be. It has been the call of the beloved. There are no more things to see. Only light. The bird that caught the light has vanished into the "Light" that caught the "bird". No form. No name. No sound.

Let us now re-visit our minds. We have tried to visualize a new model, but this is not just another paradigm shift on the extending path of enquiry in material science. It does not admit a new definition, for definition needs words. It does not lead to a new equation, for equations need symbols and symbols are condensed from words. Are we saying that words cannot deliver? In a way, yes. But in the same breath we are proceeding to say that words do contain, in the deeper recesses of their innermost intimations, the potential for such deliverance. They form the ladder that will facilitate the assent all the way to the roof, but not provide the platform to stand upon. What else was the scheme? The latter stops one step short, but enables the climber to set one firm foot on the roof. Then he lifts himself up, and the ladder has fulfilled its ordained purpose.

Science must awaken to this reality. It has begun to do so. Physics has outstripped the whole saga of Darwinian evolution with just one rarer species, the Schrodinger cat. (Bioscience may claim it has gone a step farther through Molly, the sheep.) The twin paradox will render one of the twins ten years younger than his dormant brother, after he has been on a tour at the speed of light for that period of time. (Physicists, why don't you start a tourism agency? – suggested name: Lightning Travels). "Wave" and "particle" are words that have punched holes through the roof of the space that contained those words earlier.

This progress of science may serve to unravel more facets of relativity, whose Time has enough time to spare, but it will not take it any nearer to the Absolute. Horizons recede for ever.

That is the problem, and the problem will not even be recognized as long as consciousness is wrapped up within the brain. Hence, be it said a thousand times by each of a thousand voices: Consciousness of the person is not the product of his brain. It is an eternal independent energy, for whose manifestation as effects brain is the appropriate matched equipment. This energy in motion is wrongly seen as born of the brain's activity.

When science looks at energy fields, it recognizes many; gravitational, electro-magnetic, radiation, weak forces, strong forces, etc. Hydraulic, pneumatic, thermal and electrical energies are allied by science to appliances to provide utilitarian benefits to aspiring humanity. The practical physicists in these disciplines are the *poojaris* (priests) who conduct worship of Energy to invoke blessings for human beings at the altars of material prosperity. They are the mediators between Energy and beseeching humanity. One may say pure science (Absolute) is reflected as the performing science.

It is the same with religion. Let scientists get this straight; philosophy is the pure science of Absolute Consciousness; religion is the applied science, demarking, how life can be lived in the relativistic frame in harmony with the higher but hidden realities, so that peace of mind, virtue, truthfulness and generosity can be nurtured. After all, this is the bedrock on which human happiness can rest. So religion has fashioned its *poojaris* (priests); has created divinities that represent the isolated verities extracted from relative consciousness; identified the tools of the trade as ritual and chant and symbols; and built temples as colleges in this circle of mental education. Blessings can be, and are being, invoked from physical energies mechanically, and from conscious energy mentally. Humanity at large is happy with this compromise.

Pure science should not concern itself with religion and initiate unholy debate; philosophers are not interfering with your work in the lab. They, like you, are probing the limits of limitation. The matter you investigate, and the energies you measure, do not volunteer to reveal themselves to you.

It is your knowledge-capability that extends itself and includes their new facets in its growing circle of the known. That circle is your mind, your consciousness. How could it be subordinate to grey or white matter called the brain?

We may say relativity is a child of the Absolute, and mind is a child of relativity. Therefore when mind ventures to talk of the Absolute, the talking is subject to relativity. Words are now summoned to confess that words cannot define the Absolute – God defined is God defiled – and this too is said in words. Mind is summoned to concede that its sense-perceptions return frustrated from their futile voyage to contact the Supreme – and this reference to the Supreme and the failure to reach are statements made by the mind using words.

Scriptural revelations are full of caution to the aspirant to beware of a quantum shift in meanings and methods. The Absolute is indicated on an unreachable shelf, its transcendental virtues extolled, but it is not wrapped up for you for hand delivery by a sales-person. No way that can be done, for it is "unreachable by speech or mind." *(Avaangmaanasagocharam)*. "It cannot be defined" *(Anirvachaneeyam)*, "It is beyond duality/relativity" *(Dvandvateetam)*.

"While sitting, it travels far away; while sleeping, It goes every where." (Quote from *katha-upanishad*–not to be sourced to, or confused with, quantum mechanics.)

But there is indeed no failure in this, no need for despair, no call for shame. The honest recognition of inherent limitation is the last step of the journey. We saw that the birds that are our words could, when inspired, fly into the source of Light. Then the bird did not remain as a bird, but the reflected light that had till then revealed to us the form of the bird merged into the source. Light remained. The shift revealed True Light to the observer's mind that had ridden all the way on the birds that were words. There the bird was disposable, but only because it had fulfilled its purpose; which was that, as a vehicle of reflected light, it should bring light into our reckoning, and then lead our gaze upwards and upwards to Real Light, and finally leave us not abandoned but empowered, to heave ourselves into Transcendence. This is more than an "event horizon", more than a mega-paradigm shift, more than the "most" of any knowledge. Even the enlightened ones struggle for words, but their compassion for aspiring mankind pushes them to be a bit untrue to their pristine perfection; they descend from Silence to sound, accommodate our imprisoned concepts, and express their experience in our words. So they use the word LIGHT of that consciousness; they say they are experiencing a luminosity that is a Presence in Itself – "The Splendour of a Million Suns" *(Koti surya sama prabha)*. It is not the heat-scum-light of nuclear activity in the solar orb; who wants a million times that? So obviously we have to extend, exceed, and even extinguish the relativistic mind to transcend into Reality, Truth, Absolute, Thing-in-itself. The same thing, God.

We can now sum up this allegory:

When Light lights light, we have God. When light lights things, we have the world.

When Knowledge knows knowledge, we have God. When knowledge knows things, we have mind.

## 15

# WHAT IS THE LENGTH OF MY SHADOW?

Between and beyond "light" and "Light" – hopefully we can now claim the dexterity of mind to handle words this way to deepen our probe – what is LIGHT? Science has asked, searched, and speculated. It has seen the theories of relativity rob time, space, mass and energy of their fixity. That left light as the sole monarch of the realm of absoluteness. Light had dethroned those four pretending chieftains, itself standing strong on two constants, namely, the velocity constant, and the Planck's constant (for the quantum of action of a photon). Faced with this phenomenon, science may have stopped in its steps, wondering if this is the outer limit of all that can be known of Reality.

It may well be. But what of it? What a tragedy if arriving at the threshold of the abode which the scientist sought through an arduous journey, he falters in self-doubt, concludes it must be the wrong address, and turns back? For in fact he had finally trod upon the threshold of relativity and touched the last veil that hid Reality. Reality is not a content of the known, but the knowledge that knows. If this is not known, the mind retreats, afraid or unable to lift the veil. That is why it was all-important that we decipher the words (that are birds). Mind imagines it holds words in its snare, but it is the words that hold mind in their snare.

We need to place the paired words of duality in direct opposition to each other, see both as right, and see both as wrong, then see both together as neither right nor wrong. Thus we arrive at the honourable conclusion that with reference to the Absolute, the Reality, the Thing-in-itself, the Unified Field, the verbal mind can only declare confidently what it is not, but cannot even attempt to say what IT IS.

When reflected light is thus left out of the equation together with all reflected images that constitute relativity, there can only remain true light preceding manifested creation, invisible and unknowable to the senses. It cannot be kin to light from fire or light from the sun; it has no elemental origin or contiguity. But it is not the primal Reality. Not as we conceive it, for we cannot credit light with self-awareness. Light (to our thinking) cannot be conscious of itself; light still needs a knower. That knower is Total Consciousness, the Supreme, the Absolute – also called God. Light is the creative impulse latently held in Total Unmoving Consciousness as LUMINOSITY, along with Time as a dimensionless NOW, and Space as an area-less HERE. It is still a state of being, not of becoming. When the movement starts, Reality has "become" the play of images illumined upon the stage of time-space. Time-space facilitates existence by location of the created objects. For them to be known, they must be covered by light. Elemental light can only render them visible or "see-able". They are "seen" by that faculty of consciousness called "sight". That is referred to as the light of consciousness. All this play of action, change and movement, has the reality that reflections can have – no more and no less.

**Question:** What am I doing in this meaningless medley of

substanceless shadows?

**Answer:** Nothing, if you believe yourself to be a shadow amongst shadows. Every thing, if you recognize yourself as the self-luminous one who is casting all the shadows, as the subject standing before the shattered glass-bits of time-space creating a myriad of reflections in a myriad of variations, the Being in truth yet the becoming in fantasy.

**Question:** Who, me?

**Answer:** Yes sir, you. That is to say, the "I" that says "me" in you. And by the same token, the "I" that says "I" in me. And likewise wherever an "I" stands up and asks the question.

**Question:** The reflections have disappeared?

**Answer:** What matters it to you that your reflections have ceased? What are you now? You are the Reality you have always been.

**Question:** What about the reflections?

**Answer:** They were unreal then as now. Their play of becomings was not your gain, their cessation cannot be your loss. You are pure Being. The body you identify with is a temporal phenomenon, the consciousness you possess is the timeless indestructible factor. When the reflection ceases, light does not cease to be. The body dies, not you; for, even now, as always, You are the I-sense of yourself centred in the conscious aspect of yourself. You are the electricity in the bulb, not the metallic filament.

Pages back we began a dialogue, starting with: "Suppose consciousness is X, the unknown factor." We were attempting to answer the problem after collecting all the data. But now we are finding that X is not in the category of data being put together into an equation. The question has turned inadmissible, like "What is the fixed length of my shadow?"

**Comment:** (as you rise up to leave): Goodness, all the wasted labour!

**Response:** No sir, no. The confusion was caused by the dichotomy of a "real" X along side the "reflected" X. Let us move on. What is the glory in spending a life-time framing an impersonal equation, when we can ourselves BE the answer! If we have progressed towards this understanding, we have not laboured in vain. Please do not walk away.

# 16
# THE WHITE HOLE

Whatever is perceived in the reflection must perforce be present in the subject whose reflection is being perceived. If the mirror holds to my gaze a tree with fruits and flowers, and a parrot perched on a bough, so must it be when I turn my gaze from the reflection to the original tree. There can be mutations and distortions in the reflection, but they cannot be inherent fallacies in the subject, they must only be the natural results of defects in the mirror. Unevenness of the surface, pitting, cracks, black spots, tinting, curvature – all these refer to the mirror, and by association appear as the perceived reality of the image; but they can never impinge upon the truth of the subject that stands unconcerned, and for ever perfect, in front of the mirror.

Scriptural wisdom talks of the Absolute as the Subject. "Being" is the state here, as contrasted with "becoming" which is the state of the relative. "Stillness" is the measureless dimension here, not needing time or space for its definition or description; "movement" is the dimension there, compulsively demanding time and space for its measurement. There can be no equating of the two. Yet a cause-and-effect connectivity must be cognizable. This connection lies in the inherent potential for reflection, which is the very nature of light. When we talk of Reality and cosmic creation, we have to search our hearts (sorry, our minds) to decifer whether we mean reality of creation or reality *in* creation. If distinguished, the former must have flowed into and permeated the latter – that is to say Reality "became" reflected reality. Of course a reflecting surface ("mirror") must be posited.

Return to the focus of this discussion: Everything resolves into CONSCIOUSNESS. Reality and relativity are other words for Absolute and cosmos. However, forgetfulness of singularity leads to the deceptive illusion of plurality. As consciousness is (how else?) Self-awareness, this illusion can arise only after self-forgetfulness. Suffice it for our present needs that we see it in this simple analogy: I am awake and self-aware. Then I fall asleep and self-forget. Then I dream, and while dreaming am me and yet not me. I remain me in truth, but am not me in the fantasy. Even so the seeds of my dream have pre-existed in my waking-state memory. Sleep, which is forgetfulness, intervenes and shows an altered image.

Big Bang is to science the beginning of the cosmos it is investigating. In the language of physics, it is also expressed as the beginning of time. The Black Hole contained the elemental energy that exploded to "become" the cosmos. This is the image in relativity.

Let us reset this eventless horizon in terms of consciousness, which is totally the observer-observed in a truer sense than the observer of physics. (Physics can only chisel the observer out of matter.) It must then be said that densely condensed consciousness was a small sphere of infinite content. Consciousness being the illuminator, we may say LIGHT in our vocabulary, (we speak of "light" of knowledge), this sphere would have to be the WHITE

HOLE, or even the White Whole if you prefer it that way. The contents would be "dark" self-forgetfulness. This is the paradoxical reversal: Black-hole of science, because it held light captive; white-hole of spiritual analogy, because it held darkness captive. And one spewed out "dark" matter, the other spewed out "luminous" mind.

Science determined that matter then evolved and spewed out mind. The other voice said it differently. One of them is right. Which one?

When the cosmos collapses, when the implosion occurs, the ego-person at the centre of reflected consciousness will forget the deluded reality of his "unreal" existence, and through that forgetfulness regain his identity with the Absolute. Time of the physicist must decide when the expanding cosmos will collapse. But mind is free of time. It can bring about its collapse (stillness) when it chooses to. That is meditation. That collapse is itself the redemption.

If science does not dismiss this as altogether silly it may see it as somewhat funny. Fair enough. That will allow us to relax and laugh. Having laughed together and taking our time – there is no hurry – we may arrive at asking: Who was I laughing at?

# 17
## Consciousness Is The Infinite Energy, Brain Is The Transmission System

Let us return to Darwin. By his indefatigable perseverance and unrelenting labour, he chronicled the story and sequence of physical bodies over millenia. He catalogued them patiently with meticulous concern for detail and established a consistent trend of progressive betterment of physical design and form, each successive change empowering the creature to adapt better to its environment and enhance its ability to survive.

Let it be noted that none of the actors in this extravaganza of the evolutionary drama had more than a fleeting presence. One flicker of the eyelid of Time, and each actor had come and gone. Endless Time ensured an endless succession of actors, *there was a continuity of the play, but no continuity of a player.* And this immense, wondrous enactment has been going on with no purpose and no witness, unless you nominate Time and Chance to the witness gallery. Time and Chance? Can they see, or say? (No chance.) They are blind and dumb. This is the scenario when the physical body-person and his consciousness are coeval and co-terminal. This would be the truth of the existence of living beings if consciousness was a product of the brain. Science swears it is.

But philosophy postulates that consciousness is a universal energy that manifests as the mind of man (or as sense perception in lower forms of beings), and the brain is the matched equipment, or matter-structure that receives the energy and manifests it – not unlike a radio, rightly tuned, receiving the electro-magnetic impulses and manifesting them as sound.

*Only one of these conclusions can be true, rendering the other false. The whole reckoning of the truth of creation depends on which of these is true and which false.* That is why I have said in the introduction to this treatise that this is the cardinal argument that stands like the unscalable Great Wall of China, dividing and opposing science and philosophy.

Let Darwinian evolution rest its case there. Let us listen to what philosophy has to say on the subject. It has refuted the claim of science that the organism called brain produces consciousness through neural impulses and chemical activity. Philosophy has emphatically stated that the brain is the power-house, not the power-source. The energy of consciousness makes contact with the brain-equipment which is the entry-point. From there the transmission lines go everywhere. The grid, called brain and nerves, is in place. In intricacy, complexity and capacity, the microchips of Computerland do not even merit comparison. Safeguards are provided as shunts and fuses to protect the equipment from overheating or blow-out.

Neurologists, through chemical manipulation, and neuro-surgeons, through physical intervention, can condition the equipment and alter the manifestation. (It is the same with physicists operating mechanical devices.) Is it not obvious that what is changed or controlled is the quality of the output, not the nature of the input? It is obvious if consciousness is an energy that is experienced ("seen") as mentation ("the light of knowledge"), but it is not obvious if consciousness is produced in the brain.

"A brief (or elaborate) history of time" cannot be expected to give insights into this riddle, because after all it can only be the history of time. The answer has to be sought in timelessness, which, please watch out, is not an eternity of time, but a paradigm shift of intellectual vision into a freedom from time. Such a perch is not available in relativity but only in Absolutism. Philosophy presents that bird's-eye view of creation, and invites us to share the perch and see for ourselves. (We say: No, thank you. I am going to the club.)

Hinduism has an ancient tradition known as *Tantra-Shastra*. The one Reality behind the creation of the universe (whose discovery is the ultimate quest of physicists) is the transcendental Absolute, self-aware, immutable, and ineffable. It is the totality of Consciousness. When it is self-moved into manifestation, its energy waves array themselves in cosmos in a form-pattern, to which Tantra-Shastra gives the name "SRI CHAKRA".

In creation, the scheme and method that have shaped the macrocosmic have also faithfully shaped the microcosmic (be it the atom). In ultimate terms, consciousness is both the cause and the content of perceived creation, and the energy that moves the universal, or the individual, has to be identical. Life-forces on the mental plane and the physical plane are divided and demarcated as so many executive authorities with specific functions and the total management is graphically depicted. Yogis who have mastered the subtlest aspects of their physical and vital life-currents have vouchsafed this information to mankind in conformity with their experiences.

For our present discussion let us leave out the spiritual seekers whose inward-directed quest engages in trying to see the suggestions of Sri Chakra as revealing physiological-psychological realities within one's own personality in its deepest inner construction and operation. This subject has been tentatively included here in the belief that neuro-scientists freed from prejudice and pre-judgement may discern in the concept of Sri Chakra a three-dimensional representation of the power-house and circuit diagrams, valid for the whole universe or for one living organism. There is identity between the Sri Chakra and the full potential of a person's body, and the correspondences of the various parts in the spinal transmission lines are explained. The physical, the physiological, and the psychological aspects of the person (being the bodily, vital, and mental functions) are co-related to the sub-stations from which the energy spreads and activates the mechanism.

Energy is regulated at the point of entry into the equipment. "How much is the energy that electricity can deliver?" is no question. Infinite, may be the answer. It is the same with the power of consciousness too. The pertinent question is, "What is the voltage the given equipment is designed for?" It may be 12-volts for a battery, 110 or 220 volts for lights and fans, 440 volts for certain industrial uses, etc. So in each individual the energy of consciousness functions with a self-regulated surge, and each person is what he is. But unlike mechanical devices which can only tolerate a limited range of fluctuations in energy and must break down beyond the range, the mind of man which plods along within relativity and mostly rests there by contentment or compulsion, has the potential to aspire to Absolutism. And when that happens, however rarely, the gifted aspirant cannot be telephoning the cosmic electrician for an emergency reinforcement in the neural wiring. Wisely aware of this, nature has designed the organism to be capable of absorbing and utilizing even an infinite surge of the energy of consciousness. We wonder that nature is so profligate. Bio-science tells us about the seemingly meaningless extravagance in cells and circuits, and the wastage in nature. Instead, we should be assessing the wastage of opportunity for which we alone are to be faulted, not nature. There is capital to buy a kingdom but we are struggling with a one-acre farm, or may be slaving on someone else's one-acre farm!

The Absolute has never denied relativity its rightful inheritance. It is there for the taking. The aspiration should be there in us. But to aspire, right knowledge must be there.

# 18
# WHEN BODIES DIE, WHAT HAPPENS TO THE PERSONALIZED CONSCIOUSNESS?

Are we saying that when I die, that is, when this body is no longer capable of manifesting consciousness, that energy which was associated with this body merges with the Total Energy? No, we are not. By that question we are asking whether the personalized ego identified with a body becomes free of limitation on death and therefore Absolute? Not a chance. Death is not a bestower of boons. Death is not a liberator from psychological conditioning. Words like Realization, Enlightenment, Liberation, *Nirvana*, *Moksha*, are indicative of transcendence from relativity into Absolutism. Death is not a bridge to cross the chasm. In truth, the relative does not walk across a bridge into the Absolute. No bridge is possible. There can only be a dissolution of dependence on this body for existence, and a simultaneous rediscovery of a continuing identity without this body. This is not a matter of faith or speculation. Do not ask me (even laughingly) whether I died recently and returned to enlighten you. If I had done that, be sure I would have returned no wiser. In any case it was not necessary, because we are all familiar with a comparable psychic state of bodilessness. We should not be asking questions about death with which we are as yet unacquainted (any complaints?), but should be re-examining the three states of personal consciousness offered by life for our experience, namely, the waking-state, the dream-state, and the deep-sleep-state. The secret of death is hidden there.

We have all had dreams. In my dream I was a person and the reality of the dream-life while the dream lasted was no less of a reality than the reality of my waking-life when awake. Though this body of mine was not cognized in my dream activity, as a dream person I had both body and mind. That may be distinguished by the term "subtle body" and the state of being awake can be termed "gross body". So after death, which means without this gross body, the psyche remains as a subtle body. Regardless of what we, wide-awake persons, may tell each other about the ethereal or vaporous or imaginary state of persons or phantoms in dreams, those "persons" inhabiting the dream-worlds have no such concepts of themselves. Did you miss anything of reality in your own presence and performance in your dream? The narration of a dream after one wakes up is not a falsehood, it is a truthful narration of an experience. And in your dream, you were the experiencer. Therefore it is clear and logical that the psychic entity that has died to, and discarded the gross body – perhaps this is what is loosely called "the spirit" in the West – has the same solidity, structure, sensing and re-acting, and mental activity in its own self-evaluation and belief – the same conviction and feel of being a total person – as we have when we are dream persons.

In a dream too we are experiencing a "physical-body-mind-conglomerate" which is the "subtle-body". There is no suggestion of unreality, or even a "lesser" reality while dreaming. All that talk is after the dream ends, when the dreamer wakes up, and looks at the dream from the stand-point of the waking-state.

Death creates a transition from a continuity of a wakeful lifetime into a prolonged dream-state. As with dreams, waking up must follow. But the old faithful familiar body, having served its purpose, has been discarded and destroyed. The same psyche must and will follow the same pursuit, true to its individuality driven by the continuity of personal desire for happiness. The old pattern must repeat itself because the quest and the methodology remain unchanged. Another body-mask and another environment must provide the next scene for the same actor.

A person dies with his quest for abiding completeness unfulfilled, but the desire-motivated psyche remains. The Law of Energy in the Universe, mental or physical, is the Law of Causation. Cause produces its effect. As the cause, so the effect. That effect is the cause for the next effect. This is causation, or the causal flow of energy. Not transgressing this Law, the psyche must now associate with another equipment, in another environment; that is, it has to reincarnate. The word is derived from *carnal* and means entering a *carnal* (flesh-related) frame *again,* re-in-carnate. The new situation or relating must be causally justifiable and correct for all the components of the new causal equation; the parents, the family, the country, the universe. For, Laws are Universal and there must be impeccable, unimpeachable correctness in the administration of the law, so that many facets touched by one decision must all receive due justice in terms of the law. No event stands isolated and unrelated. A birth is an event that includes the new-born, the parents, and all else. In this causal correctness is imbedded the factor Biology calls heredity. The causal demand is that the converging streams of consciousness – on one side the newly arriving psyche, and on the other the on-going parents – must be so aligned that there is complete rightness in the assemblage. When the mental aspects and needs are thus coordinated, it is a natural secondary consequence that there will be correspondences in physical aspects too. The primary cause is in matching the streams of consciousness; one of the resultant effects is matched physical factors. These may include "inherited" facial features, and may include also asthma and arthritis. How else can it be? DNA is not the mechanic, it is the tool. But science reverses cause for effect. Science will suffer those hiccups as long as it swallows the fallacy about brain *producing* consciousness, and then that has to stick in its throat!

This rightful matching of personal purpose to cosmic propriety takes place so naturally and beautifully because in truth consciousness is one total unitary Absolute and all events always and everywhere are its own thought-impulses. There can be no thought unknown to consciousness or unrecorded in it. Please read the Bible again where it says: "Not a sparrow shall fall, but my Father knows." The governance of the Universe is run by one cosmic computer, self-programmed and unerring. The Programmer and the Program are synonymous. Call it the LORD or call it the LAW. You are welcome to your choice of word, it makes no difference. The much-totted convolutions on the surface of the brain are only the print-outs. The contents are determined by the computer, not the printer.

These erosions are like the grand canyon of Arizona which is an amazing, but natural, recording and result of the persistent flow of a river. The energy and the history belong to the Colarado River and not to the plateau. The ancient history of the psyche that has laboured through many vicissitudes has sculptured the geography that the neurosurgeon witnesses in the physical brain. The un-conscious, sub-conscious, and current levels of the psyche have their circuits already laid out in anticipating readiness. What should surface can surface, when needed if needed. The impact of the past is inherent in the present.

This brief narration on the vast and complex problem of reincarnation is incorporated into this treatise essentially to emphasize the limits of theories of evolution which only catalogue the changing body-forms in their temporal sequence, and have no need for a continuity of conscious unfolding through a linked process. Refuting this, and delegating such evolution to its rightful *secondary* status of providing the altered equipments to match the demands of altered manifestations of life-energy, the wisdom of the science of consciousness (not starting, but ending, with the brain) reveals Nature's methodology in *primary* terms.

As this teaching, being subtle, can easily be misconstrued, an amazingly perceptive exposition of the intricacies of this vexed mystery has been bequeathed by Sri Aurobindo, the world-renowned Yogi of Pondicherry, in *The Problem of Rebirth*.

In his inimitable style of flowing phrases and cascading thoughts, the great master and mystic erases the easy and popular conception that it is John Robinson who "went" and John Robinson who "returned". He says the evolving psyche is not the same pillow stuffed into another pillow-case, and decries it as a vulgar conception to assume soothingly that there is no birth of a new soul-construct at all, but only the birth of a new body for occupation by the old personality. Who "leaves" and who "enters"? There has to be a continuing identity, but there *cannot be* a continuing person.

This identity is built into the methodology because the content and intent of every stream of seemingly individualized psyche is flowing from the unitary totality of consciousness. This totality is a persistent immutable reality, but, as with the subject and its reflected image, the totality is other than myself, other than this composite that I call myself, centred in the I-am-this-body belief.

Only when there is clarity about the Absolute and the relative will the word "immortality" reveal its true and attainable significance. Time for the physicist is not a parameter for immortality. Time may refer to eternity, as mathematics refers to infinity, but both these terms are pretensions. As for bioscience, it has locked consciousness in time-spans of brain-cells. It has got its bearings wrong on mortality, so what sense can there be for it in immortality? Beings and meanings acquire a mutation across the border of transcendence, and there familiar words shine with an unfamiliar luminosity. And, thus, it is said that only he who goes from personality to PERSON becomes IMMORTAL. Sri Aurobindo would have us know that the "ego-person is only its distorted image reflected in the stream of embodied mentality."

The long voyage of ego-life in its multiple probes and varied moods is only the movement on the surface, as waves upon the ocean. The foundation on bed-rock is the past experience held back from the physical memory. Therein lie the nuances of identity and continuity.

# 19

# THE CONTENT IN CREATION
# AND THE INTENT OF CREATION

Science can investigate the wakeful-state and the dream-state, because these are manifested states and available for observation. Qualitative descriptions and quantitative measurements are possible in the world of objectivity. In the wakeful-state the psyche is witness to the phenomenal world of cosmic creation; in the dream-state, the same psyche is witness to a world of its own creation. That is the only difference. The commonality is that the observer is there.

*But in the deep-sleep-state that observer is not there.* By definition, this is the thoughtless state. There are no thoughts, that is, no activity of consciousness. We may say in comparison with the other two ego-states, this is a non-ego-state. If the wakeful-state is the "gross-body" state of physical existence, and the dream-state is the "subtle-body" state of mental existence, then the deep-sleep-state is the "causal-body" state, potential but not kinetic. The scientist probing consciousness sees a void here, more or less. (There may be the slightest suggestion of a linkage, retained like a key to the house lodged in the pocket of the owner to facilitate a return.

82

Deep-sleep permits retention of the key; death takes the key away, and that is no big deal as the house is demolished.) Seeing the void the scientist closes the file. True, he has understood the operative mechanics of the brain. But he has not understood consciousness. He believes he has.

The causal body is the potential stage of any energy. It is the seed-state in which the energy is at rest. What will re-emerge is what retracted into seed-form. As the seed, so the tree. As the tree, so the seed.

The psyche which was active while wakeful, and loitering while dreaming, is restful in deep-sleep, but certainly has not ceased to be. The continuity of personal identity on waking confirms an unbroken existence. And as the dormant psyche was the occupant of the deep-sleep segment, it was not a void. There was no object of perception, but potential awareness never ceased to be. As there can be no hole in pure space, there can be no void in pure consciousness.

So through dream or sleep or death the individuality persists, with a momentum of its own making. The limited and conditioned mind, seeking abiding happiness beyond want, keeps following the wrong methodology. The desire-oriented logic suggests that such fullness and perfection will come in time, if only one persists. It will not. There was a man standing patiently on the sea-shore. He wanted to enjoy a swim in the sea, but he was going to wait till the waves subsided totally. A wrong approach cannot yield the right result. That man is still standing there, waiting.

This correction of method and then an easy return to the pristine original state, is the scope and sense in the play of consciousness. Earlier the question was raised whether it was scientific to talk of any purpose in creation, and to whom purpose and fulfilment could refer. We have tried to indicate the answer. Consciousness and intelligence are like the sun and its light and cannot be conceived in isolation. Therefore creation is an expression of intelligence and not of inertness. There has to be a meaning, a method and a purpose to creation. The movement is from a meek acceptance of limitation back into the freedom of the unlimited. It is a personal voyage, but an ordained one, with no option for the destination, but with a choice of the route. As long as the journey lasts, so long must there be the continuity of temporal-spatial existence and experience. Equipments (bodies) wear out or break down. Environments grow stale or sterile and turn unsuitable for the charted advancement. Therefore the functional purpose has evolved a natural causal continuity, for which re-birth is the methodology.

Science cannot easily come to terms with this. That is so because science knows everything about the CONTENT of creation, but nothing about the INTENT in creation.

"Intent" here is not to be read as the will or purpose of an inscrutable "God", and God read as a locus outside creation, shaping it arbitrarily. Let "intent" mean a law of consciousness that ensures a continuity of causal flow so that the end is a return to the beginning, all the movement is sequential, and nothing is random. Intent is the infallible rightness in the Law. If a God is posited as the law-giver, he is the Law too. We can be comfortable with commitment to LAW. I dare say GOD would then be equally comfortable with such an understanding on the part of the scientist.

At this stage we can only invite scientists to compare and contrast the doctrine of Darwinian evolution with the doctrine of reincarnation, and assess which of these penetrates superficial observation and at deeper levels agrees more closely with reason and logic.

"Evolution" is the right word, but evolution of body-forms is the *consequence;* the *cause* lies in evolution of the psyche that inhabits the body-forms and uses them as the vehicles on its journey.

Modification of bodies is secondary, modification of the inhabiting consciousness is primary. It must be understood that *homo sapiens* did not board the coach of Time on the last leg of the journey. The entity that is the man of today has been on the band-wagon of creation from the start, though evolving and changing form along the long voyage. Whichever body-form seemed to the psyche to incorporate the best design and idea for preservation and progress, has been possessed, used, and later discarded as inadequate. The history is forgotten but its condensed impress is there in the present body and mind. Therefore, oh man, fin and fang and feather you have played with; claws and canines have served you; ferocity, hugeness, sinew, speed and cunning were your faiths that promised but failed. Nothing gave you mastery, for the elements cannot be mastered. The solution lay elsewhere, it lay in the mastery over mind.

This recognition has been achieved by man and therefore his essential need or demand can no longer be further evolution of body-form. He need not grow wings to be an angel – if aerodynamics permit – for angels, like him, (I am told by humans) are beings with minds. Man, as he is, can aspire to escape from the gravity of relativity into Absolutism. The body is no longer the block. The block is in the mind, and can be surmounted.

Evolution has been a long and arduous journey. DO NOT SAY MAN IS THE FINAL PRODUCT OF EVOLUTION. He did not jump on to the wagon one halt before the final destination. MAN IS ALL OF EVOLUTION. Evolution is not a relay-race in which man ran the last lap. It is a marathon, and he who finished the race is the one who ran it all the way.

⚘

## 20
# THE WANDERING MINSTRELS,
# ONE LAME, ONE BLIND

The zealots of science and of religion have both mellowed or mutinied – hard to say which – as the new-age thinking (already aging) caught the physicists with confusing contradictions and the preachers with unsustainable, even intolerable, dogmas. The worshippers of science, practical men of the world that they are, toiled in their laboratories (cosmos being the prime one) and emerged with altered perceptions and honestly said as much. The worshippers of spirit, soul, mysticism, ethereal heavens, transcendentalism or divinity, fearing the tightening noose of their own vague verbosity, found the fire-escape in the new diagrams of reality drawn by quantum concepts. Some physicists hesitantly went along a little way, partly to be polite, partly to hedge an uncertain unfoldment of the frontiers of knowledge; but the men of "belief" and "faith" went to town with "observer and observed". They comfortably concluded that the Subject-Creator and His free-willed objective-creation had been set in proper sequential perspective. To them, God had thus declared Himself through the penitent physicist.

Let the resultant resounding rapid-fire tamasha (Mardi Gras) tour the world and fill the book-shelves. It is as though two civilizations, with two opposing cultures, inherited a common set of words with identical pronunciations but conflicting meanings. The two societies may talk to each other, sharing familiar sounds and feigning communication, but can only get as united thereby as two stone-deaf good souls sharing the park bench all afternoon. Let the high-priests of physics, who do not think this is funny, clearly recognize that it is the preaching religionist, like the drop-out researcher, who is making such untenable claims. We have distinguished earlier in this book pure science from applied science – philosophy from religion. We will stay with the true philosopher, call him seer or sage or saint. Call him the mystic who for himself sees nothing mysterious. New-age writers trying to clarify mysticism are actually drowning it. The greater lament here is that their own discipline will also drown with it, because two non-swimmers caught in a current and locking arms for support will end up disabling each other, not supporting. The good news is that there is (has always been) a redeeming factor. While scientists navigate the ocean of relativity through sun-shine and storm, the Enlightened Knowers of Absolutism are manning the watch-towers of Reality. They are the life-guards who will not allow science or religion to sink. They are alertly in position. The swimmers can swim as long as they choose to – their passes are valid to eternity. But if they wish to reach the invisible shore, the hand is lovingly held out. The chick within the egg knows somehow when its time has arrived, and starts breaking the shell from within to come out of its captivity into a freedom unknown but instinctively sensed. It is then that the mother hen, if she considers it necessary, helps the release by aiding the cracking of the shell from outside. That is the inherent law of Nature.

Till such time, it is far more prudent and practical to accept the simple reality that science probing material phenomena, and religion defining moral, ethical, aesthetic and compassionate attitudes of mental states, are two different aspects of our existence, experienced by humanity without mutual conflict or mutual accord. There is no call on any one – just any one – to forge an alliance between science and religion and force them into wedlock.

It is understandable that a great scientist who was also a great humanist, speaking with more modesty than precision, and wanting to be more amicable than analytical, once said famously: *"Science without religion is lame, religion without science is blind."* This quotation has done the rounds globally, and, in a way, that is good, for it cools the tempers, heals the rashes, and leaves an aura of profound conciliation. But, for all the deep respect and admiration I have for Einstein, whose this edict is carved upon a century's intellect, closer scrutiny reveals it as a homily, no more. And I say it with humility. Half-truths have their use in leading attentive listeners to higher truths. Einstein has here spoken of religion, the waters that spread across the vast fields of human behaviour and irrigate them to bring forth the utilitarian flowers and fruit of ethics and morals; Einstein, by design or chance, has not talked of philosophy, which is the mighty torrent, turbulent here, serene there, deep deep everywhere, flowing between the banks of Absolutism and relativity.

If may also be pointed out that the symbolically stated infirmities of religion and science should have better been transposed, because one would associate vision with religion, and mobility (or momentum) with science. Einstein was obviously indicating a degree of imperfection in each entity, rather than meticulously diagnosing a disease. Still, I would be less uncomfortable with lame religion and blind science, than the other way around. Then, the inherent strength of each discipline would be intact, while the supporting strength would be missing. This edict declares that both religion and science are essential for humanity, and that one without the other would be paradise lost. Let us put them together practically and pragmatically. The lame one has sight, the blind one has legs.

The lame one shall therefore sit astride the blind one, and now the twain shall travel. Lame science will see and call out the direction and choose the terrain, blind religion will obediently walk the path. Where will they (or it) go? My question is, whereto will this manipulated accord take humanity? Will a new goal emerge out of this wed-lock? Will Reality be born out of this consummation?

Let us not take comfort in soothing phrases. Creeping about individually both will fall into their alloted pits individually. If they team up piggy-riding and march as one unit, the two entities will still fall into the pit of limitation together. Take your choice. There can be compassion for the handicapped in the relative frame of creation, but that cannot extend to giving them entry into the Absolute.

Philosophy knows that here and now is the ultimate destination. The voyage, if only you know, has ended where you are standing now. Lacking legs is not the problem, lacking (in-)sight is the problem, but science refutes that. Science wants movement to track movement, science wants time to unravel time. So it roams the vast vistas of relativity, and that is exactly what our piggy-backing comrades will continue to do. There is no solution here.

Mankind acquired rockets and satellites and roamed through space the way mere aeroplanes could never have done. Someone came back from his orbit and confided that heaven and God do not exist. Now we have it on his authority. But was that indeed humanity's problem, and, if it was, has it now been solved?

❧

# 21
## PEBBLES ON THE SEA-SHORE

Science is terrestrial. Religion is also terrestrial. There is nothing called celestial as a theme apart. Men discuss angels; we do not know that angels discuss men. What has meaning for us – and it has paramount meaning – is the dichotomy of "the relative" and "the Absolute". Man has the right to ask the question and the ability to answer it, because all knowledge is the effulgence of consciousness, and consciousness has to have for its source and sustenance I-AM-ness, and man has it. In fact my I-AM-ness is even now the Absolute. Include "relative" in it, if that is the way you want to use words; no harm done; you would have made the superfluous statement that you insist on including all numbers in your infinity, and all temporal sequences in your eternity. Why! That is the only way it is, and can be, even without your having to say it in so many words.

Let us share a dialogue that Nisargadatta Maharaj, the great sage of India of recent vintage, had with visiting westerners and others. Such visitors were serious, mature seekers enquiring into the depths of spirituality. They plodded through dust and din and environment unfriendly to their sanitized senses, to find the unpretentious Nisargadatta Maharaj in a cubby-hole of a dwelling in Mumbai that was Bombay. We can envy them. Diamonds are concealed under encrustations, pearls lie hidden under sea-weeds. It takes commitment, endeavour and persistence to uncover and claim such wealth. Those that stayed awhile with Maharaj returned rich.

For enabling the spiritually less-initiated to tune in with the wave-length of the following broadcast, it is necessary, to point out that every Master on this plane of enlightenment has declared consistently "I am not this body, not just this person you see seated here, not an ego-centric individuality. You will tend to believe it cannot be otherwise, as you will judge me the way you judge yourself. But you are limited by relativity. I am not." Here may be simple words you know too well, but with meanings you have not known so far. Therefore, the need to pause and meditate leisurely. Now, to the dialogue recorded on 12th October 1970 in the book "I AM THAT." (published by Chetana Pvt Ltd, 14 Rampart Row, Mumbai)

**Question:** You seem to be a poor man facing problems of poverty and old age, like everybody else. You are experiencing pleasure and pain.

**Maharaj:** I am experiencing it in consciousness, but I am neither consciousness nor its content. I do not see the world as separate from me and so there is nothing for me to desire or fear.

**Question:** So we differ. Your experience is so different from ours.

**Maharaj:** No, we do not differ. The difference is only in the mind and temporary. I was like you, you will be like me.

**Question:** God made a most diversified world.

**Maharaj:** The diversity is in you only. See yourself as you are and you will see the world as it is – a single block of reality, indivisible, indescribable. Your own creative power projects upon it a picture and all your questions refer to the picture.

**Question:** A Tibetian yogi wrote that God creates the world for a purpose and runs it according to a plan. The purpose is good and that plan most wise.

**Maharaj:** All this is temporary, while I am dealing with the eternal. Gods and their universes come and go, avatars (divine incarnations) follow each other in endless succession, and at the end we are back at the source. I talk only of the endless source of all the Gods with all their universes, past, present and future.

**Question:** Do you know them all? Do you remember them?

**Maharaj:** When a few boys stage a play for fun, what is there to see and to remember?

I invite science to pause and re-examine its adamant investment in evolution, having convinced itself that the physical-psychological-intellectual composite will extend its parameters till some distant future reveals the original uncaused cause and its ultimate fruit. As scientists you are nominating Time for the highest honours. You have branded consciousness the imposter to the throne of Reality and locked it up in the material prison of brain-cells. The illusion is in science, not in philosophy. The benevolent call of the Sage to the sceptic echoes the plea of Shakespeare's Hamlet, who cries from the hurt in his soul to his misguided mother as she tries to hide behind a shield of self-righteousness,

*"Mother, for love of grace,*
*Lay not that flattering unction to your soul,*
*That not your trespass, but my madness speaks."*

Try not to be suspicious of being misled or tripped by some "sage" whose credentials are unverifiable by you, but search for the deeper clues in the seeming irreverence of the Master's audacious disclaimer of "gods and universes" as a temporal play staged "by a few boys for fun." Note that gods (in plural) refers to manifestations that are qualified and temporal, and therefore within the frame of relativity.

"I" is the anchor and mind is subservient. The mind serves my chosen purposes. I have so structured my mental identity that I need a remembering mind for my continuity in time. And I need time and space for my playful extravaganza. So I have linked memory to linear time, and made the mind a repository of temporal sequences available to me for recall and response. We use the word 'God' for the 'creator', and the word 'world' for 'creation.' One word has to signify Reality, so the other word can only signify relative reality, also called reflected reality. I-AM-ness has to be recognized in both the frames. Therefore it may be said: THE WORLD EXISTS IN MY MEMORY. GOD EXISTS IN MY PRESENCE.

# 22

## SUBSTANCE AMONGST SHADOWS

Science is about signs. Science is tracing the foot-prints and finger-prints of energies that have chased matter relentlessly and continue to do so. Science interprets the signs discerned through telescope and microscope. Through the ingenious language of mathematics it creates its own "signs" or symbols to reduce the findings into recordable equations. The study of events involving matter in space and time yields the laws of physics, formulated as comprehensive principles, and expressed with economy and precision as mathematical equations.

The progressive clarity in the vision of science has sharpened its definitions of subject and object, of observer and observed. This is far removed from a hasty (and convenient) interpretation in some quarters, both religious and scientific, that there has been a blurring of the division. Eminent physicists have warned against such "misuse of language" as Louis de Broglie calls it. Shroedinger stood his ground and said that the fuss on "pulling down the frontier between observer and observed was a provisional aspect without profound significance."

Ken Wilber declares that "the physicist is looking at nothing but a set of highly abstract differential equations – not at reality itself, but at mathematical symbols of reality".

Bohr has said physicists are dealing "with a purely symbolic procedure." Sir James Jeans has said their "final harvest will always be a sheaf of mathematical formulae... our studies can never put us into contact with reality." Eddington has categorically asserted that the search for reality by the methods of physical science leads only to a *"shadow world of symbols"*.

Ken Wilber in "Quantum Questions" writes: "In perhaps the most famous and oft-quoted passage of any of these theorists, Eddington eloquently states: 'In the world of physics we watch a shadowgraph performance of familiar life. The shadow of my elbow rests on the shadow table as the shadow ink flows over the shadow paper'."

Well said, but half-said. For, the question immediately arises: "Whose elbow, what table?" It is not enough – not at this level of deep perception – to say "my elbow and that table", for evidently "my" would here posit the scientist, and "that" would refer to a material thing. Both of them, as entities in the physical world, are matter. Science has reduced the entire world of matter to shadows; so you are now saying that a shadow casts a shadow. Does it?

I grant Mr Eddington did not mean it that way, for he has hedged his utterance, and gone on to say "there must be more behind... we return to our starting point in human consciousness – the one center where more might become known." But this statement can be meaningful only if consciousness in not seen as a product of brain cells – if it were, then consciousness is in the same frame as all the symbols and shadows you talked of. If science has not given it a symbol, it is because science has not given symbols to love or hate or hunger either. Science has not only refused to see consciousness as an independent energy, it has not seen it as anything at all to merit even a symbol. A painting has a man standing and casting a long shadow. Does the canvas support the painted man one way and the painted shadow another way?

In the frame of relativity, which includes all that is, or can be, sensed, the sensing consciousness of the individual also has only a relative reality, because it is (as we have seen) "reflected consciousness", and does not possess the Reality of the Absolute. The "I-am"-ness in the ego-person is intrinsically the same as the I-AM of Absolute Consciousness, but in the relative frame of reflected consciousness, there is a falsification due to conditioning by time-space coordinates. That automatically qualifies and quantifies the I-AM center, limits it with a circumference, finds space for any number of bubbles within an expanding sphere, and invites measurement of their interplay.

When the inherent limiting nature of relativity is annulled, signs and symbols have no relevance and erase themselves. The false ego-sense of the perceiver who was created by the process of perception, the false entity of a subject that arose coeval with objectivity, cease to be. Duality dies. The unreal ends. The Real remains, self-asserting.

Thus is the Absolute frame indicated using symbols (words) which are the tools of the relative frame. Words of our spoken language have at least some flexibility, but words of the language of mathematics do not have even that. How then shall we capture Reality in our equations? I am glad, so glad, to have Einstein himself standing up to answer this question with finality. He has said, "As long as the laws of mathematics refer to reality they are not certain, and as long as they are certain they do not refer to reality."

The mathematical mysticism of Pythagoras declared: "All things are numbers." He should have said, "All that can be numbered are things." Measurement is inevitable in relativity, but it is impossible in the Absolute.

So you will permit me to say that science is only about signs, but science does not know who signed the cosmic document that science is reading and researching.

Still there is no need for despair. True, science cannot reach God; but equally true, **the scientist can.**

# 23
# WHO AM I?

Einstein and Hawking amongst physicists of the past century are generally regarded as extraordinary luminaries. (There could be a few others.) Likewise, Ramana Maharshi and Nisargadatta Maharaj stand tall amongst those seen as enlightened souls. (There are others.)

The majesty and grandeur of Ramana Maharshi – 'Bhagavan' (Godhead) to his adoring and grateful devotees – was in the simplicity and directness of his teaching. Someone said it succinctly: "The *acharya* amplifies, the sage simplifies." (Acharya means teacher of spirituality or religion.) Ramana Maharshi, the great Sage, stayed unswervingly upon the core centre of spiritual enquiry, virtually standing tip-toe upon a dot. And that dot was the single question: WHO AM I? For a seeker coming to him for instruction and guidance, there was no escape thereafter, no plea for more time, no search for more mental space, no sequencing of causalty. The "I" in each one is so undeniable, so imminent, so persistent and so evident that you cannot elude the question you are called upon to answer to yourself: WHO AM I? The Sage was focussing your attention on the truth of your-self, the Reality that knows only the Here and the Now, the pure state of consciousness as Existence, which is I-AM-ness. He would say: Know Who am I? 109 this and all else will automatically be known in right perspective. (With apologies to Shakespeare, taking some liberty with the famous counsel that Polinius gave to Lacerates:

*This above all, to thine own Self be true;*
*And it must follow, as the night the day,*
*That you cannot then go wrong within relativity).*

You are not the body. You are not the mind that is only the record of your body's history of sense-play. You mistake yourself to be the time-bound conscious one. In truth you are much more than just a conscious one – YOU ARE CONSCIOUSNESS.

In the words of Ramana Maharshi: "You must distinguish between the "I", pure in itself, and the "I"-thought. The latter, being merely a thought, sees subject and object, sleeps, wakes up, eats and thinks, dies and is reborn. But the pure "I" is the pure being, eternal existence, free from ignorance and thought-illusion." The mind is thus coaxed by the Maharshi to make the paradigm shift into this understanding first, and into its experience later; from reflected consciousness to Absolute Consciousness; from relative reality to Reality.

❧

# 24

# THE ACHILLES' HEEL: TIME FOR PHYSICS AND BRAIN FOR BIOLOGY

We have been looking at physics as the study of matter and elemental energies and at bio-science as the study of organisms and vital energies. Philosophy has derived that Consciousness is the unified energy, but science resists, if not derides, that inference. We have to say that the "brain" is the Achilles' heel of biology; and proceed to consider whether "time" is the Achilles' heel of physics.

We have already seen that mind (of which each one of us has personal possession and experience) is a flow of thoughts, and a thought is a movement in consciousness. We have also seen that Total Consciousness is Absolute and we cannot talk of movement there, any more than we can say that space can go for a walk – there simply is no outer space into which space can go for a stroll. And yet our minds are real to us and the flow of thoughts in ourselves is not hearsay or conjecture, but the assertion of experience. This seeming reality is "relativity" as distinct from the Absolute Reality. Mind's quest for Truth has perforce to be confined to the limits of relativity.

The mind is familiar with instances of illusory reality where the nonexistent seems to exist. The blueness in the sky, the voice in the echo, the world in the dream, and the view in the mirror are false assertions but totally credible. Thus it is with the sensed reality in creation. Therefore mind must be distinguished as *reflected consciousness*. Nothing can move the sun, but by catching the reflection of the sun in a bowl of water and shaking it I can make the sun dance. By muddying the water, I can dim the lustre of the sun. By pouring out the water I can proclaim the death of the sun. But the true sun is beyond events. So is it with Absolute Consciousness, and the illusion of relativity.

To see this is to see that the universe which is being investigated, *and those that are investigating it,* are equally the projections of a *relative reality*. And it is in this frame that time claims reality for itself. Relativity is founded in perception. "Thought" is the basic unit, its flow is the process of knowing. "Thought", we have seen earlier, is a construct of consciousness, assembled from the subject-component "I", and the object-component "it" (the thing), to become the moded knowledge of a thing. "I" is the "particle" when at rest, "I" is the "wave" when in motion as mind. A "thing" is existence in time and space. Thus time becomes fundamental to thought. But the energy of thought (the movement) cannot be the contribution of time, it must evidently be the contribution of consciousness. It follows that "time" does not move, it is *moved*. It is a dead-weight riding piggy-back on me who is at the centre of consciousness, and it has tricked me into believing that it, as time, is the energy that is running my life! "Passage of time", indeed! It is passage of thoughts in me that creates the illusion, as when I look out of a speeding train, the trees seem to be running.

That is why it is said in the study of consciousness as energy, in the deep-sleep-state time does not exist, because there is no movement of thought. The ego-centric I-ness of the person has become still and therefore time too has become still. *Stilled time is killed time, for it has no causal energy of its own into which it can recede.* But stilled psyche is not a killed psyche. Being a movement in total consciousness, it can rest unmanifest as causal potential. That is its seed-state. On being returned from deep-sleep to wakeful awareness of itself, the psyche re-creates time.

By definition deep-sleep is a state of thoughtlessness. Each thought is a wave of moded consciousness. When this moding and wave-movement is taking place, the paradigm is of reflected consciousness in which the ego-I gains its relative reality from time and space, and endows its false reality on time and space. (What a comedy, like a bankrupt doing charity on unsuccessful borrowing! But before we can usefully laugh at ourselves, we need to take ourselves seriously; so let us continue tracking the ego-person, my "I" in me, and your "I" in you.) When a thought-wave has subsided, and the next one has not arisen, it is a thoughtless state, the same as deep-sleep state. To the ego-person there is no "state" there, it is nescience or the negation of consciousness. So it is a void. But then, the statement itself is void, because the existence of the "person" who might have a say there, is itself void.

The reach of relativity has ended there, because mind (which is thought-flow) has ceased to be what it was, or more accurately, what it seemed to be, in the waking and dream states. But the Absolute Consciousness never had boundaries. It was the Reality behind the reflections and remains untainted and unaltered by the appearance of reflections or their cessation. It is the only Reality equally pervading and cognizing all the three states of the ego's waking, dream, and deep-sleep.

We have seen that the waking-state and dream-state are periods during which the person is cognizing thoughts. In the deep-sleep state the person does not experience thoughts. It is the thoughtless state. There the mind has stopped, and therefore time has stopped. On waking up the person senses the interval between the event of falling asleep, and the event of waking up, and that creates again the recognition of time; but during deep-sleep there was no time.

Now let us look at a thought, which is the unit of consciousness. A thought arises, exists, and subsides. Then the next thought arises, exists, and subsides. After the subsidence of one thought and before the rising of the next thought, what is the prevalent condition? It is the thoughtless state. It is the causal state, potential but unmanifest. For the ego-person this is the state of nescience, a void in consciousness. The personalized I-ness of the psyche is suppressed, but it has not perished. The seed sprouts as the next thought. *So, with the rising of each thought, the psyche recreates both itself and time.*

The nescience or void described above, is in terms of the individual consciousness. It is true with reference to the limited ego, but it is falsified when seen in terms of the unlimited. *Consciousness cannot countenance nescience, any more than the sun can see darkness.*

To understand thought-waves, let us turn our observation to water-waves upon the surface of the ocean. What is the reality between two waves upon the ocean? *The ocean, is it not?* The wave is moded water, the form is the shape, wave is the name. The wave is not other than the ocean, and can rest nowhere but on the ocean; it is not a thing apart. When the divisive mind of the perceiver has individualized the wave and given it a separate identity, keeping the attention focussed on the wave has amounted to missing the ocean. But the indispensable substratum is always the ocean. That is why it has to be said truly that between the waves lies the ocean.

The sages have similarly guided our enquiry into the right

focus. When asked "Can you show me God?" Ramana Maharshi replied "Yes, look between two thoughts." So simple? Yes and no. Yes, because the mind is complex, though God is simple. He is so imminent and intimate, yet not recognized. No, because when you attempt the seemingly simplistic solution, you find to your chagrin that "looking" means having a thought of the cognized, and in the attempt to discover a gap between two thoughts, you have actually deposited a thought there! You find you cannot "look" between two thoughts without closing the gap with a thought. The observing interferes with the observed.[2] This conundrum leads to the understanding that the relative cannot gain Absolutism while insisting on its own terms of relativity. The meaning and method of meditation to arrive at Reality, to gain enlightenment, must be defined and formulated with this clear understanding. It is evident that activating the mind (generating another objective thought) is not the right approach. Only total subsidence of the mind is. In the case of the individual we have seen that the state of subsidence of thought is the state of deep-sleep, a negation of awareness. This cannot be enlightenment, or spiritual progress! No aspirant is so dumb as to believe that deep-sleep will carry him into liberation. So nescience and void are words that describe a state of the created person, not the changeless state of the Creator. The I-ness of limited, conditioned, personal consciousness – the ego – coexists with objects, being itself an object of creation. But Total Consciousness, which is the creative energy, is Self-Awareness, and when I-ness refers to it, that is Reality. That is the Absolute.

In deep-sleep, when all thought-waves have subsided and consequently the ego-sense too has become submerged in ignorance of itself, it remains as the causal potential. With it, the conceptual time-space remains integrally as the creative potential. That potential belongs to Total Consciousness and not to the partite ego-sense. A reflection does not appear, move, or disappear by its own will or energy. The cause for all that happens to the image

---

2 *Physics makes a statement with the same words, but not with the same understanding.*

lies in the subject that is reflected and is not shared by the image. At that point, when we may say that the Creator's foot is raised but has not yet landed in creation, time with Him is a dot called NOW, and space is a dot called HERE. There is no duration when time is seen as NOW; there is no area when space is seen as HERE. Therefore when the mind, which can never be free from time-space conditioning, tries to visualize Reality, it has to state that Reality is "beyond time and space". That is to say, while the "person" believes by force of habit that past and future are really distanced from him, the only experience of time that I as a person am having, or can ever have, is in the present. Obviously, when I think of the past, that thought (recollection) is experienced by me NOW; when I think of the future (projection), that thought is experienced by me NOW. This is the eternal operation of mind, so an eternity of time is contained in the NOW. Similarly an infinity of space is contained in the HERE.

We have been examining "time". When subjected to the critical test of conscious experience, the time we have believed in is a fable, for there is only the residual dimensionless "present". And even the existence of that residue comes into question. Let us look into that also, and totally lay bare the fallacy of time.

This "present" moment or occurrence has a connotation of personal experience that is special to all of us. What makes it so? The quality of time, as eternity or as the present instant, should be the same. Yet there is a difference. Let us listen to the brief, beautiful, brilliant exposition by the sage, Nisargadatta Maharaj.[3]

*MAHARAJ: Surely, a memory of the event cannot pass for the event itself. Nor can the anticipation. There is something exceptional, unique, about the present event which the previous, or the coming, do not have. There is a livingness about it, an actuality, it stands out as if illumined. There is the "stamp of reality" on the*

---

3 *I am That; Publishers:* CHETANA PVT LTD, BOMBAY - 23

*actual, which the past and the future do not have.*

**QUESTION:** What gives the actual that "stamp of reality"?

*MAHARAJ: There is nothing peculiar in the present event to make it different from the past and the future. For a moment the past was actual, and the future will become so. What makes the actual so different?*

*OBVIOUSLY, MY PRESENCE. I am real, for I am always now, in the present, and what is with me now shares in my reality. The past is in memory, the future in imagination. There is nothing in the present event itself that makes it stand out as real. It may be some simple periodical occurrence, like the striking of the clock. In spite of our knowing that the successive strokes are identical, the present stroke is quite different from the previous and the next, as remembered or expected. A thing focussed in the now is with me, for I am ever present; it is my own reality that I impart to the present event.*

Thus, on enquiry, linear time is not linear, being only the "present". Time is a dot that cannot be launched to leave a trail. And even that dot is occupied by ME, not by time. So the "present" in time is also demolished, what survives is "PRESENCE", the I of Total Consciousness, the Absolute Timeless Reality. It is this that has been given the name GOD – this and nothing else. Any objections?

BEING is this stillness in Consciousness, the ABSOLUTE state. BECOMING is that movement in consciousness, the RELATIVE state.

BEING does not admit time. BECOMING cannot occur without time, for "becoming" is a process, a movement, requiring an interval of time. Time is a descriptive word for the way the process of change and flow is experienced. The experience is in consciousness. Time is the measure of the movement in mind, and the mind is mine. God (Absolute, Being) does not need a mind; time, (insentient vehicle of becoming) cannot have a mind. But I, the deluded fusion of consciousness and body, a being in flux in an eternity of becomings, cannot be without a mind.

The scientific temper is respectfully requested to be more circumspect when it refers to "the mind of God".

"My mind", we all say. Who am I that possesses the mind? Who am I, the possessor, apart from the possessed mind? That I-ness is the endless substratum for the ever-changing mind. But the I-ness I claim for myself as this person, now making these wise (or otherwise) verbal statements, is emerging out of the ego-sense of the mind, and is therefore a case of mistaken identity. The real experience of my own I-ness is what is called Realization or Enlightenment. As a man, I have identified myself totally, inseparably, with the body. Because of this transgression of the truth, *mind is man's cross and he is compelled to bear it*. The cross is non-transferable. He must bear it till he is crucified upon it. The fundamental error is nailed down, to perish. The error perishes but not the I-ness. That does not perish, it cannot perish. Only the shadow of reality is nailed, not reality. There is then the resurrection, the transcendence. "I and my Father are one" is not an assemblage of duality, but a seamless fusion; the Totality of Consciousness, not a fragment called mind. Even calling it a fusion is not correct. Nothing is correct when the sound symbols of relativity are super-imposed upon the Absolute. When the reflection ends, what in real terms has merged or fused with the subject that caused the reflection? To have believed in duality was the error. It was the first error and has remained as the only error all along. That is the "forbidden fruit" that created mentation, and mentation (relativity) prevents repose in a paradise (Absolutism).

❧

## 25
# NO BRIDGE TO THE CREATOR,
# BECAUSE HE IS RIGHT HERE

I am nearing the end of my narration. Maybe presumptuously, or maybe purposefully, I have opted to walk upon the "razor's edge". For one who ventures thus, the only protection to the sole can be humility in the soul. But humility is not an assessment one can make about oneself. At the end of the day, the mere fact that the soles are not bleeding proves nothing; the deluded professor may not have even been near the targeted area, wandering witless in distant barren lands, far removed from the razor's edge. And comfortably cosy in self-esteem!

I am not a scholar, my span of attention is too brief and wavering for scholarship. Science was my subject in college, but I was an indifferent student, never deferential towards differential calculus. Philosophy touched me quite late in life. I had no background, tradition or preparation that equipped me for such study, but its intimacy and immensity in personal terms captured my interest. I have not had, nor have I sought, opportunities to move closely in allied circles, but my nature remained contemplative. In later years

I found it necessary to write down the stirrings in my mind, as it was the best way for consolidating, condensing, and retaining the conclusions of my progressive quest. Authorship was incidental, self-education was my concern.

I lay no claim to technical perfection in my statements in the realms of physics or bio-science. However, I do not perceive that any such lack of precision need be an obstacle or a disqualification to this attempt at persuading the scientist to see a valid extension to his own frame of study, which is not only rational and substantive, but also the absence of which can render his frame flawed or, at the least, incomplete. I seek the indulgence of the scientist to correct any aberrations of dots and dashes in my presentation, and to render perfect *in his own reading* my diffused statements *on his speciality*, and then relate the corrected and more accurate construction to what I have down-loaded from the site of philosophy. The scientist will find that the holistic logic will hold just as well (or fail just as ill). If someone has written a good poem, we need not throw it away because of a few mistakes in spelling. If it is a bad poem, correct spelling will not save it from the dustbin.

The statements made by me as signifying the philosophic concept of consciousness and time and the causal methodology in creation, are not *"original"*. In the West, intellectuals who have thought deeply over morality, justice, behaviour, social order and communal harmony, or have rationalized observations of cosmic phenomena and the energies of Nature, are credited with propounding philosophies, different and "original". But there are other and truer stars in the firmament of knowledge that are basically of a different persuasion, for whom, strange as it may sound superficially, NOT TO THINK would be the highest application and attainment of intellectual prowess. To stop the process of thought and witness the superceding state of consciousness is their methodology for enquiring into creation. Such stars of human endeavour are there amongst Hindu sages, Islamic Sufis, Zen Buddhists, Christian mystics and Jewish masters. Their fulfilment did not reach culmination through observation, but through *inner experience.*

AMONGST THEMSELVES THEY ARE WITHOUT DISSENT, WITHOUT DOUBT, AND WITHOUT DIVISION. That unified voice is the offering of REALITY or REALIZATION to humanity. That truly is philosophy. It is ONE TRUTH, in all climes and at all times, in all languages and all societies.

Never mind that this unity is missing globally in humanity. Religion is meant to be philosophy applied to the practical business of living, providing an ordained way of ritual, worship, conduct and kinship, so that the ultimate goal of love and transcendence is not lost sight of. Religion should be the undercurrent of civilization that surfaces as the spring of philosophy. But it has been natural to humanity over the ages that ideals are distorted, ideas are corrupted, and the face of truth is smeared with falsity. Science should not hastily pick up GOD from the rubble and ruins of religious practices, prejudices and perversities, and pass cursory judgements on philosophy. If earnest, one may critically examine the Pure Science of Absolutism that philosophy alone has mastered.

Physics does not tread so much upon the toes of philosophy, barring when half-humorous references are made to God – with a rare snide remark thrown in for flavour – and we can forgive ourselves our trespasses. After all physics is studying the reactions of inert matter to inert forces and no feelings are involved. Neither the strangulation in a Black Hole, nor the ferocious explosion of a Big Bang, wounded a body or a sentiment.

But it is a different and indeed a more serious matter with bio-sciences. Convinced (as blue-blooded scientists tend to be) that this God-business is all a mental mode and foible, they focus on discovering the linked environment within the brain that would rationally explain many states of cerebral and vital oddities.

They explore, and sometimes rightly expose, claims of trances, "materializing", levitation, clairvoyance, or suspended animation. The investigation is praiseworthy. But, in the first place, who said these phenomena, true or false, were proofs of the presence, power, and potency of whatever is called God? How much of multifaceted creation is revealed to the sensory gaze of science and how much still awaits discovery? If what is seen and known is not yet an indicator of the inherent errors in the logic that says we can catch the creator amidst the creations by widening the vistas of investigation, and if this does not provoke us to suspect and re-examine our methodology, it would be a case of our running perpetually towards the horizon to catch the rainbow there. By all means study all reports of the unusual, the abnormal, the unbelievable, and assert the conclusions of rational, scientific investigations. Enlarge the understanding of relativistic computations, even as physics recently altered old doctrines into the refinement of quantum concepts where the truth of matter at one and the same instant could be both a wave and a particle. But do not project that it has somehow brought us closer to the Absolute. Truth does not move progressively on a linear scale from relativity to Absolutism; no more than numbers added progressively can land in the lap of Infinity.

There is no bridge that the investigating mind arrives at, to cross the anticipated chasm from creation to creator. THERE CAN BE NO BRIDGE BECAUSE THERE IS NO CHASM. Distance is not the dividing factor. Whatever is qualified and quantified is mortal, and mental; and therein lies the disability.

I fear that some bio-scientists assume that probing the neural status of "practising" "god-men", willing to oblige with command performances, will reveal cosmic origins. It will not. But it should reveal more intricacies in the equipment called brain that can manifest hitherto unsuspected nuances in the energy of consciousness. The frame of relativity will be enlarged and embellished. The Absolute remains aloof, perfect and total. Why don't we leave it alone?

There has been mention of neuro scientists enlisting claimants of *"yogic"* prowess for studies on their brain activity or repose. It is appropriate that the scientists first study the deeper significances and subtle variations of words like trance, *yoga, pranayama,* and *samadhi.* They are technical words, prone to corruption in common usage.

Any system of regular religious or devotional observance or prayer is a discipline and therefore an act of concentration of mental energy. Being channelized, it becomes more powerful, and may manifest *siddhis. Siddhis* are unusual and normally unsuspected high-voltage potencies of consciousness, accessible to anyone who persists with the right technique and determination. But Reality is about transcendence of the ego-person, quite the opposite of fattening the ego with an enhanced sense of domination and doer-ship. Realization means absorption in Reality and that is the gift of self-enquiry which ends duality.

A *yogi's* trance is called *samadhi.* While it is a sublime state for the person, it is not the end of the personality. Even if thought has ceased, the potential is suppressed and not sublimated. The state is conditioned by time and the ego-sense will return. It is like a bucket of water let down by a rope deep into a well. It is submerged and not isolated, but yet retains a partial boundary, because of which the bucket of water can be pulled out. Similarly the mind in trance can resurface. On the other hand, the mind of the sage in the *Sahaja* (natural) state is like a river that has joined the sea; it knows no return, and admits no separation. That *Sahaja Samadhi* is Reality. The state cannot be ascertained by observers who may witness closed eyes or frozen body or vacant look or speechlessness or abstinence from activity. Yet, in contrast with ourselves, it is the ego-less state.

The soaring thought of our Rishis, in the rarified realms where intellect glows with intuition, has bequeathed to us words of brilliant import that can take us beyond words themselves. They are the last holds for the aspirant before he hauls himself into Reality. When relativity ceases, words have to cease. So there are words which are luminous planets of knowledge orbiting the sun of wisdom. Let us not mistake them for fireflies in the dark firmament.

It is with this apprehension of misplaced exuberance that I caution against a casual trespass into the preserves of "samadhi".

I have stated earlier that a scientific study of mental activity must go beyond the states of wakefulness and dream, into the deep-sleep-state to pursue the psyche to its origin. The I-sense, which is the persistent irreducible minimum of personal existence, is not traceable in deep sleep but returns intact on waking. Where did it reside incognito? Wherever,  it had a border with the experienced world.

The relentless pursuit of the fugitive reveals that consciousness of the individual has yielded place to nescience in deep sleep, and that has negated current experience, and yet has not negated the continuity of the I-person. It is therefore a void, but there has to be a beyond to it where the I-sense could remain unmanifest and manifest again. (We cannot say the I-sense was in the void, for, then, the void is not a void.) This is the Egoless State of Absolute Pure Consciousness. It does not belong to the world-order to which the three states of waking, dream, and deep-sleep belong. These three states exist in, and as, reflected consciousness and are seen as experienced by the reflected I-am-ness. Therefore the Absolute has been called the fourth state, *Turiya*. It is not a state like the other three really, because it is not exclusive. Rather, it is all-inclusive. A man and his three reflections do not make up four men. *Turiya* state alone is real and the other three are merely false appearances. For this reason, the word TURIYATITA (surpassing the fourth) is also used, for added accuracy, and refinement of the concept.

Can the scientist accommodate this in his present understanding? Please pause and ponder.

So what is it you are going to probe when you chart and measure the processes of the physical brain during various states of stress or stimulus?  And to what will your findings refer? Was it the humility of genius, or the genius of humility, that spoke when Einstein said:

*"As far as the laws of mathematics refer to reality, they are not certain; and as far as they are certain, they do not refer to reality."*

With these words Einstein propounded a more profound, a more accurate, statement about Relativity than his equation $e = mc^2$.

&

# 26
## AM I CREATURE OR CREATOR?

I started this narrative with the statement that the great divide between science and philosophy, over centuries past, has been the assertion of science that brain-matter produces consciousness, while philosophy asserts that consciousness is an energy that functions through the brain (which is the matched equipment) and manifests as the mind. This book has been an attempt to expound upon this statement.

If the statement is essentially wrong, philosophy gets thrown into the rubbish-heap. All is matter. There ends the matter.

If the statement is essentially correct, science does not get one wee bit devalued, it will only be more rightly circumscribed. The brilliance of scientific investigation into the structuring of hydrogen and carbon or organic cells, the penetrating gaze of the scientist into the cosmic wilderness and into the atom's heart, the extrapolated rationale projected from present observation into milleniums past or yet to come – all these attainments will retain their glory and utility.

But in the altered frame of perception, the nebulous concepts about an unknown creator yet hiding in a mostly-known creation will be addressed. The scientist will know that the enquiry into that millionth part of a second which triggered the Big Bang, is still an enquiry into creation and not into the creator. And that the probes into the brain are an exploration into the labyrinth of tissues and nerves of the complex equipment, but not into consciousness. By changing brain biochemistry, we can never change consciousness. All we can do is suppress particular symptoms and prevent certain manifestations of the energy. If we can laugh at ourselves without taking offence, let us share this little story. A man was driving his aging car, with his little son by his side. Suddenly he tensed up. "Oh, oh, trouble for sure!" he exclaimed as he came to a halt. "What is it, dad?" asked the kid. "Son, the engine is heating up. See that little red light on the dash-board? See, it has started glowing." "Dad," said the boy, "why don't we pull out the red light and keep going?"

If the search is for the ultimates, neither philosopher nor scientist can arrive there until and unless he pauses in his outward gaze and turns it inwards to focus upon the I-centre in himself. Each one of us, conscious entities that we are, has his I-centre. The I AM is primary, and its I KNOW is secondary. Creation consists of the WORLD (known through perception), GOD (a postulate for the first cause) and ME (the I-person). World, God, and ego (I-ness) together constitute creation. They appear together and disappear together in consciousness. "God" is included as the instrumental cause for the manifestation of the world. It is the postulate of the ego-mind and must be included in the frame of relativity. When the word "God" refers to a mental projection, it is the stuff of the mind and not Absolute, just as a perception of "infinity" cannot be isolated from our mental structuring of numbers. No idea can cross the boundaries of relativity; ideas and the words that carry them must both perish upon the border. But when "God" becomes invalidated as objective knowledge, it acquires reality as subjective experience. This is so because Consciousness is eternal and everything including the "I" in the relative frame is, has been, and has to be in truth the "I" of the Absolute. So when rationalists scoff at the gullibility of lesser mortals and assert that man created God in his (man's) image (as a pallative or an escape–route), we will not object, but we will point out that they have reasoned well only within the mindset of relativity. The failing is not that man speaks of God, but when will he take off from that springboard to realize that there is a transcendental dimension called the Absolute, *beyond words but within experience?*

The world is untroubled and unconcerned, being insentient. God, whoever, has no questions (or He wouldn't be God). It is me, this I-person, who has all the questions and all the problems. Questions and answers are not arising by themselves, they are not external, they can only have a locus in me, in my I-am-ness. I am at the centre of all that is known to be. So what does it make of me? It raises the all–important question:

*Am I a creature (created being) or am I the creator?*

If my ego-sense of I-ness is the crux of consciousness, and if consciousness (like any energy) is forever and not limited to the time-and-space-frame of one bodily existence, then evidently *I am coeval with creation.*

Such a prompting from the bio-scientist would immediately impact upon the physicist, for the question can be translated into: *Am I in time or is time in me?*

In fact we have determined not two, but three, locations for I-ness, and correspondingly, Time also acquires three distinct perceptions.

*First:* Biologically structured, I am a creature in time. I am a tiny unit in creation, a bubble upon a foaming ocean, and my life span is a brief instant in the vastness of time.

*Second:* Freed from the misconception that my I-sense owed its birth, function and demise to a brain in a body, I go beyond the limited destiny of one body-form, which means beyond death, and gain the attribute of eternal. It means that I possess the temporal expanse that Time itself possesses. *I am coeval with time.*

In this frame there is the identity of my I-ness with eternal consciousness in the kinetic mode. There is creation, there is play of energy on matter, and there is time as the facilitator of creation, for (as we have seen) the generative thought that moves omnipresent potential Consciousness into waves of mentation has to be Time-Space. In this frame, "I" am no longer the Lilliputian but the Gulliver, the energized Creator, and time has been conceived by me and rests in me. It is my tool and my play thing. It is not the master and I am not its slave. As my pet doll of a dog has a tail, so this time has an appendage called death. It cannot wag its tail unless I make it do so.

*Third:* Beyond all this lies the Absolute, Pristine Totality of Consciousness. Words cannot reach there, nor thoughts, nor sense perceptions – which is to say, they are not valid in the Absolute, having been structured for relativity. Only one word-sound may be smuggled into the serene, supreme Silence of the total "space" of Consciousness. That word is I. It is not really the *word* that transmits, it is the *experience* of I-ness that is already possessed. But since the word "I" stands diluted and discounted in our usage, signifying the puny ego-self, shall we agree that I need (or "I" needs) another word? That word is GOD. *I am beyond time.*

What is time in this third locale? It cannot be accommodated. Time was linear in creation, time was a dot in the creative concept, but time is irrelevant, impossible, in the Absolute. *So an eternity of time yields to the timeless eternity.*

As a layman, looking bewildered at the outstretched arms of all-embracing physics, I vaguely wonder whether the barrier to the unified theory lies in the complexity of time – linear time of phenomena, spiral time of memory (observation can never be free from the conditioning of memory-recall), and dimensionless time at the "event horizon" of the creative concept. (Beyond that it becomes non-existent time, like the "fourth" state of *Turiya* we discussed earlier).

I learn from Stephen Hawking's *A Brief History of Time* that St. Augustine pointed out the fallacy of imagining God as a being existing in time and corrected it by declaring that "Time is a property only of the universe that God created." I doubt if this made sense to physicists. Shall we evaluate these words of deep insight in the context of what we have just discussed? It means that creation is relative and needs the time factor, whereas the creator is "God" and time has no entry there.

The scientist is carrying a quiver of arrows to string his bow of intellect and hunt down Reality. He is armed with the thermodynamic arrow of time, the psychological arrow of time, the cosmological arrow of time – and perhaps a reverse arrow of time. Perhaps an arrow of "imaginary" time. But every-time he will miss the target. He will not bring home the prey. If he is truly blessed, he (the ego-I) will be preyed upon by Reality (Total-I). That alone is worth praying for.

The Theory-of-Everything when enunciated, the unified Field when tucked into an equation, must yet remain statements or symbols of the world of inert matter; they cannot encircle the totality of creation, because they cannot include the functioning fundamental factor of consciousness. (We are of course talking of "reflected consciousness", a relative factor. Absolute Consciousness is immune to our speculations.)

How will science structure-in consciousness? It is the framer of the equation, but it has to be framed into the equation. How? Further, time is of the essence of the problem. Measured time of physics flows differently from psychological time. Psychological time serves memory, scientific time serves measurement. Psyche and time start from a dot which is the "present", flow into the "future" which is forward, and continue to flow in reverse into the "past", and create "memory" there as a potential causal mode. Every perception of the psyche views the new "present" experience offered by the "future," through the window of "memory". Memory conditions and colours every perception – the new is a modified expression of the old. This continuous operation of time has the geometry of a spiral and not of a straight line. Without this play of time, there would be no memory. Without memory, we are not. You are not, and I am not. What remains? Pure Psyche, if you like – psyche without psychology. Another name for the Absolute! But then we have lost our frame of relativity. Can science include spiral time in its equation? Otherwise the scientist will be standing outside creation and describing it – he will be playing God.

27

# ENTROPY AND MATTER – WHAT ABOUT ENTROPY AND MIND?

Physics has a quantity called entropy which is a measure of the degree of disorder of a system, and it has postulated a universal law that decrees that the entropy of a closed system always increases. If mind and matter (consciousness and brain) constitute one closed system – as bioscientists assert and physicists do not deny – maximum entropy in the system would have to be a state in which matter and mind are both totally decayed and disorganized. It can be said that matter has then hit the *bottom-line*. But a mind that is quiet, still, and silent, has hit the *acme* of its potential. It has been the cardinal point of this dissertation that mind is a movement superimposed upon Total Consciousness, as waves upon the sea, and when the movement, which is thought-flow, subsides, pure and pristine Consciousness remains as perfection. This is not intellectual speculation, for, in the science of Self-Realization, this has been propounded, practised, and *verified through experience* by sages during millenia past.

Is it not a paradox that you declare mind and matter as two faces of a coin, yet when you toss it one face hits the ceiling while

121

the other hits the floor?

It would be a hilarious paradox – it would have to be – if brain was producing consciousness.

But it is not a paradox, because what is seen in association with the brain is *only reflected* consciousness, and when a mirror is shattered it is only the reflection in it that is shattered. The death of the ego-person, who is the I-sense seemingly centred in "reflected consciousness" of relativity, has no mourners, because that "death" is itself the re-affirmation of the Reality as the I-AM of Absolute Total Consciousness.

If you must, enter spiritual discovery through entropy.

Physics has understood that there is a point in the phenomenon of a created universe where all theories based on fundamental assumptions break down. Such a point is called a SINGULARITY. Events before the singularity cannot carry consequences into the time-frame after the occurrence and therefore physicists would say that time had a beginning at the Big Bang, a singularity. That is how they define and describe time for mathematical reasons.

But the larger import of this rational deduction is that causation, which is the cause-effect sequence, and fundamental to law and order in creation, cannot spill over a singularity. If time had its beginning within creation, it follows that so did causation. How then can we posit a creator outside creation, or identify a first cause, and helplessly ask again what caused the first cause? When we do that, we are deceived into the fallacy that the relative can discuss the Absolute absolutely! Sorry, we can only discuss it relatively. That we are doing so is borne out by our intellectual outreach "to know the mind of God," or to analyse whether God decrees and retires or persists with the management, whether God pushes or pulls. If you ask, "Why did God create the world this particular way?"

there is no answer because the question is patently inadmissable. "Why?" is causation-hunting. Any answer to any "why?" starts with "because". Right? Well, because is be-cause, meaning "cause being so". You have said prior causes, if any, break down at the singularity. How, then, are you framing this question?

I have the deepest admiration, and respect approaching awe, for this legend named Stephen Hawking. His physical courage, his moral strength and stamina, and his honesty in conviction and expression, make him an embellishment to humanity. Though I lack the background preparation to understand adequately his *A Brief History of Time* (in spite of his compassionate rendering of the subtlest in simple terms), I have looked through the book repeatedly, and I think I sense, though not grasp, the scientific perspective. I am grateful, but I wish, I so earnestly wish, that these concluding comments had not been authored by Dr. Hawking. Towards the very end his book reads:

"Up to now, most scientists have been too occupied with the development of new theories that describe *what* the universe is to ask the question *why*. On the other hand, the people whose business it is to ask *why*, the philosophers, have not been able to keep up with the advance of scientific theories. In the eighteenth century, philosophers considered the whole of human knowledge, including science, to be their field and discussed questions such as: Did the universe have a beginning? However, in the nineteenth and twentieth centuries science became too technical and mathematical for the philosophers, or anyone else except a few specialists. Philosophy reduced the scope of their inquiries so much that Wittgenstein, the most famous philosopher of this century, said, 'The sole remaining task for philosophy is the analysis of language.' What a comedown from the great tradition of philosophy from Aristotle to Kant!"

A middle-aged woman walked up to the judge with a meek-looking man in tow. "Judge" she said, "this man and I have been married for twenty years. This dispute between us has to be resolved. I will tell you my side of the problem." And she proceeded with her brisk narration; the judge listened patiently. Then, with hardly a break, she continued, "Judge, now I will tell you his side of it." That is where I left the scene. Evidently she would proceed to say: "Judge, you can see clearly that he is in the wrong." And then go on to pronounce what judgement the judge should pronounce!

As one saint smilingly told a questioner in a similar situation, when philosophy was rapidly, relentlessly and unilaterally sought to be denigrated, "How quickly you yourself accuse, prosecute, judge and convict on your own evidence!"

As science rests secure in repeatable and reproducible *experiment,* so philosophy rests secure in repeatable and reproducible *experience.* At the core, philosophy is rationalized extrapolation, followed by anticipation, followed by experience. That is the confirmation. The event is communicable. The complete narration, guidance, and even exhortation has been there for longer than long ago. Philosophy is not an infant aged two or three millenniums. Intellectuals may have helped to change diapers! It is the men of realization, the truly enlightened ones, that have held and adored the ever-smiling Eternal Child. Since time has no entry there, the Realized Truth can be described as the Eternal (Ageless) Child. Since that is the state of unbroken bliss, it can be thought of as ever-smiling. The sages of Self Realization hold up that Child to our gaze. Are we interested?

How can Mr. Wittgenstein (glad to make your acquaintance, sir. I have not had the pleasure before), presented by Dr. Hawking as the most famous philosopher of this century, say: "The sole remaining task for philosophy is the analysis of language," when philosophy, deeply committed to identify what is the ultimate answer to all what, why, where, and how, has so clearly stated the centrality of silence in relation to sound (words)? It is not the silence of the grave-yard, the zeroed energy of maximum entropy, but the power and strength and source of all expressions of sound-syllables that are languages. In the scripture of my land – and I believe it must be the same in the true scriptures of all lands – Silence is contemplated at the level of Absolutism. From that Silence issue forth four levels of sequential stages to form words: They are *Para, Pasyanthi, Madhyama, Vaikhari;* Equate them, in the idiom of science, with unmanifest, nascent, conceptual and manifest.

1. In the Absolute frame the potential for sound is Silence. Since that Absolute state is called God, our word is Silence there. That is *Para,* which is Absolute, Undifferentiated Consciousness.

2. The creative ideation has to be acknowledged since we say God created. "Let there be light" is one way of saying it. Search it out in the Bible. "I will become many" is another way. Find it in the Vedas of the Hindus. In that concept, Silence is transformed into nascent Will which is yet to crystallize into thought form. That is *Pasyanthi.*

3. It crosses the border (that is no border) at the singularity and then it is mentally graspable sound. It is vibrating in the reflected consciousness of the ego-person. It is the thought-form of the words. It is *Madhyama,* that is to say, the middle position, because Para is outside the reckonings of relativity and so the next three only can be numbered. *MadhyamaVak* is the stage of middling Word that can be mentally heard.

4. Now the emerging word becomes gross. It can now relate to the gross instrument of matter, called brain, which sends impulses to the material vocal chords to produce the vibrations. Lo, the articulate word is born! What is born is the fourth generation of sound, Vaikhari. And will Mr. Wittgenstein (we just met, sir) appoint philosophers to baby-sit with them?

Space is what emerges first when we reconstruct elemental evolution, for there has to be space and only then can elemental air, fire, water and earth be located. Space is the first, and its "property" is sound (vibration). So the first or primary component of manifested creation is vibration, which is sound, which is the word (language). Creation starts there. (Let us avoid a distracting argument by agreeing that Big Bang is also only a big sound).

Throughout this writing I have refrained from quoting scriptural declarations, but now, troubled by the flippant intransigence of science in its reference to philosophy, I am proposing a peep into the hidden luminosity.

Let the Western world, considered to be the custodian of the scientific kingdom, look at its own Bible with less cynicism and more openness. Let them search out (never mind, read St. John, Ch-I, Verse I) where it says.

"In the beginning was the Word, and the Word was with God, and the Word was God."

The timeless wisdom of the Vedas, the precious inheritance of mankind, has spoken thus:[4]

"This, (in the beginning) was only the Lord of the Universe. His Word was with him. This Word was his second. He contemplated. He said, "I will deliver this Word so that she will produce and bring into being all this world"."

"The Word is infinite, immense, beyond all this….. In the Word all the words find their support."

"The Word, imperishable, is the Firstborn of Truth… hub of immortality."

---

4 *English rendering by Raimundo Panikkar in "THE VEDIC EXPERIENCE" published by "ALL INDIA BOOKS," PONDICHERRY*

The implication of these scriptural texts, when translated into scientific reckoning, is that when the Absolute is seen moded as the relative, that is creation. Essential thereto is the emergence of primary space, for, where else will creation rest? So the Absolute is postulated as saying or conceptualizing or willing: "Let there be Space"! But the Absolute ("God") is Consciousness, while Space is elemental and inert. Space is the medium, while the purpose is self-expression. Science knows that sound is the corollary to space. "Vibration" in the Absolute has meant the creation of space and sound (and the category of time as frequency). Consciousness can now "relate" as the biological fulfillment through the "sense" of hearing. This is the evolution of the creative energy, flowing in two streams, "matter" of the physicist, and "life" of the bio-scientist.

Whether we call it the inner incandescence of intuition, or the explosive intelligence that could not be contained in "knowing" but had to consummate through "becoming," that is what distinguishes a sage.

The reward the sage offers to humanity is not an extention of knowledge but the kingdom of Peace.

Philosophy is the quintessence of such revelations of the ultimate, bequeathed to us through indicative pointers while words of accustomed usage are made to strain against the habitual meanings in their struggle for expression at the frontier of transcendence. Fables and fairy-tales and fantasies, parables and *puranas* exist in abundance and serve humanity nobly, for they preserve an expansive base for the mass-contact of humanity with higher strivings, and in time lead mankind, even unknown to itself, towards higher ideals and happier societies. But we do not expect Science to make an unholy mix of mostly the gross with slightly the sublime, and write an equation for God. Adults do not read Shakespeare through comic strips.

❦

# EPILOGUE

I am writing these words in July, 2001.

The brief but significant episode in my life that has ended with the writing of this concise book started for me in January this year. World-renowned Physicist, Stephen Hawking, was in India, participating in "STRINGS 2001", an international conference to discuss the "string theory" which had become a focal theme for new physics and related mathematics. In a popular presentation of higher physics to an intelligent but lay audience, Hawking's reference to "God playing dice with the universe", by itself an admissible pointer to the probability function of quantum theory, caught media attention and raised giggles or eye-brows.

As a student-seeker looking for consistent meanings on the science-philosophy border, I had something to say on the argument.

I do not know which unseen hand pulled the "strings" for me then! An article I wrote was published in a leading newspaper, and was noticed in certain quarters of eminence, resulting in my being invited to participate in a high-profile event "CONSCIOUS 2001", a conference on "facets of consciousness." It was mainly organized by "The National Brain Research Centre." A few American and British Universities also had deputed scholars, and even computer scientists had claimed a slice of the cake to include Artificial Intelligence. They apparently had one seat for a mind-less one and I filled the bill! To me it was a boon, for I had long been contemplating the irreconcilable differences in the perceptions of bio-scientists and philosophers regarding brain and consciousness, and now I could make a statement in the appropriate forum.

My chance to learn from and share in these two circles, my trespass into the higher reaches of physics followed closely by admission into the labyrinth of brain-mind caverns, gave me glimpses of a complementary role for these two distinct sciences, physics and biology, to focus understanding upon the ultimate answers. Time held the last secret of matter and mind the last secret of life. Without a fusion, both would be lost!

I had to expound on this for my own edification.

It had seemed that Time had enthroned itself for eternity and gratuitously given a measly three-score-ten to mind. On enquiry, mind (consciousness) owned the throne and Time was only suffered by default.

Death was never born, and life never died.

After these brave words, I know what is in store for my body. At 76 I have already received bonus of 6 years. But I can happily borrow for my future epitaph this delightful verse of an unknown author:

DO NOT STAND AT MY GRAVE AND CRY.

I AM NOT THERE. I DID NOT DIE.

That is the undeniable truth of my – and your – identity in the temporal-spatial frame of relativity.

But of those that have "arrived" at Absolutism, and if you and I have not (I know I have not), it is only because of self-imposed self-perpetuated limitations by oneself upon oneself. Of those that the world sees as Enlightened, or Realized, or Liberated, the declaration has to find an idiom suited to transcendence.

Ramana Maharshi is one such. He is my master, my inspiration, my proof of purpose and possibility. It was 1896, and he was sixteen, when he found himself experiencing the quantum leap into Reality. It was 1950, and the body was seventy, when it "died".

Of Him I can only say:

LONG BEFORE TIME COULD WRITE RAMANA MAHARSHI'S OBITUARY,

RAMANA MAHARSHI WROTE TIME'S OBITUARY.

What follows is the section added as a supplement to this new (third) edition of "Dicey Problem of New Age Science". It contains contemplations and comments that arose in me on reading "Code Name God" by Mani Bhaumik (Physicist; Co-inventor of Laser), Published by Penguin Books.

GOD,
HOUSE NUMBER ZERO,
INFINITY ROAD,
CREATION.

# CODE NAME GOD –
# AUTHOR'S NAME MANI BHAUMIK

"Dicey Problem of New Age Science" was originally written in 2001. Couple of years later, when a reprint was due, it happened that I read Ken Wilber's "Quantum Questions" which led me down valleys and up cliffs that I had not envisaged in my survey. The newly visited mist-laden vistas held my gaze; the seen mist, the half-seen interwoven shadowy suggestions, the waiting-to-be-seen reality behind the translucence. The material sun shedding its subdued rays even now upon the mist would lack penetration to unravel the scene in its full and pristine majesty – the linked progression of scientific enquiry had its inherent limitations of relativity. The revelation could be complete only in the luster of the sun of Absolute Consciousness shining through the mist from yonder beyond – that intimation of spirituality alone had the potential to dissolve the mist. A sense of the nothingness of all things spoke to me more intensely using old words with new meanings, and I eagerly wrote them out. Thus a few chapters were added to the original text to enhance, deepen, or clarify what had already been said on the same theme. I remain grateful to Wilber for the clearer and more candid probe into which he moved me by framing questions that science could neither ignore nor satisfactorily answer.

It is now October of 2007. A couple of months back it fell to my good fortune that I bought a copy of "Code Name God" by Mani Bhaumik. To science and technology he is the co-inventor of LASER. To me he is a spiritual heart hooked on to a scientific brain, aptly symptomatic of an innocent Hindu village kid from a mud-floored hut in India, later ensconced in splendid mansions of marble and crystal in the United States of America. The hut lives on in his nostalgia while the person is blighted or blessed to live on in the mansion. Through his memory hums the background monotone of spirituality; through the intellect vibrates the high-pitched material probe of science.

I like the book immensely. No wonder, I like the man. Part of the book is about himself, a self-introduction, without aplomb or apology, without pride or false modesty. Blondes and bachelors make a heady cock-tail, and high velocity covers up the empty space. (Male and female – proton and electron?) Bhaumik has a right to say it all, and he says it rightly. Anyhow watch him closely and catch the wink! The man has wit.

Then there is the larger part that is science, which places one like me much in debt to him. There is depth with clarity, and restraint for the good of the reader who likes to know the outlines clearly but need not comprehend the details within the outlines. Bhaumik is delightful in marking the sign-posts and mile-stones on the journey of physics towards the promised(or presumed?) land of Ultimate Unity or the First Cause.

The third part of the book has Bhaumik sitting in his hut and staring at his palace – and slightly mixing up metaphors. From bullock-carts to Rolls-royces he has ridden them all, and the village-boy in him continues to sing through every outing. And the scientist in him remains convinced that the end of the road will take him to the end of space; that linearity will end the mind's quest; not that the mind must abandon linearity. I have admiration and affection for this phenomenal countryman of mine – I, like you dear Bhaumik, am a country-boy gone to town (a small town though) – and I am not faulting him. In fact he is the inspiration and happy instigation for my writing these lines now and I am beholden to him. I am only compelled to hark back to what I have been saying and make my statement more clear if I can, and answer all the new defense evidence of science in summing up the case of spirituality. I can see that the earlier conclusion still stands and even stands more fortified in its rationale. It is not *my conclusion* in any personal or exclusive sense, it is only my *understanding* of what seers have said since times unmarked, like the first man who wanted to walk to the edge of the flat world, and walked and walked, and when he found himself home again without a reversal, had to grin sheepishly and knowingly and concede and confirm that the world was round; how then could it be flat?

And our question (flat or round, having been mercifully resolved) now is whether consciousness, which we individually know, and *by which* we know, is an effervescence of matter, which it must be if it is a neural output. Brain, like the rest of the body, is also molecules, which are matter. Is brain the *equipment* through which consciousness manifests, or the source? Bhaumik ends his narration of two hundred thoughtful pages saying that "the Universal potentiality of consciousness that resonates in the individual mind is the power behind all existence, the power of the *one source* that unifies all fields and forms, *as well as consciousness*". His concluding words are: "It will not, by now, surprise you to hear my assertion that we call this source by its code name: God". If that is the source, the First Principle, the Unified Field, then concede, Dr. Bhaumik, that God is an equivalent word, not a protected code. The word does not matter. What matters (any pun is unintended, or unavoidable) is that the energy as field mutates or evolves or grossifies into matter, given as much time as time alone can give.

No hurry, but how can matter claim to be the structured source of consciousness? When mind wants to confront God, when relativity wants to peep through a key-hole in time at Absolutism, it is like the son wanting to be present at his father's wedding.

The idea of God is not herein ridiculed. We are not face to face with an impossibility; only with a misunderstanding. Mind needs to be revisited. By the mind; who else is there that can do it?

# From A to Z

This is not intended as a statement about the English alphabet. It is a pleasant coincidence that the first and the last letters of the alphabet suit my purpose to emphasize the singular unwavering assertion of all deep contemplations of spiritual import, of all climes, and of all times.

Let A denote Advaita, the non-dual reality of, and in, creation *(God defined is God defiled)*. Let Z denote Zen, that uncanny blend of rationalism and intuition, a conveyance of reality through indicative knowledge and instruction that exposes all limitations of mental prowess, strips the mantle off words and wraps it around the shoulders of silence. ("The instant you speak about a thing, you miss the mark")

When they have stopped speaking our language, Advaitins and Zen masters are both speaking the same language. And this is true of all the seers, who, men turned sages, no longer propound "schools of thought". We may have to say that theirs is the single school of *thoughtlessness*. Included therein are Islamic Sufis, Christian mystics, Hindu sages, the Buddhas, the Rishis, all seemingly personages but in truth beyond personality.

Sanskrit, the ancient language of India, preserved in my country in scriptural text and religious tradition but no longer the spoken word of the masses or the classes, yet being acclaimed by the computerized intellect of modern genius as being the best organized system of consistency and coordination between sound and meaning across the whole spectrum of vocal communications called languages, has coined the word ADVAITA as the ultimate expression of reality, for the one Truth of all. Dvaita is duality; therefore A-dvaita is non-duality. It is a negative statement. It had to be, as no positive statement would be right.

How so? Because our lives are totally experienced between opposites. In our understanding or experience, in emotion or sensation, in perception or transaction, every category of life is quantized and quantified, measured and coloured. Every category is linear and there is no central point, or any asymmetric location, to one side of which is the positive and to the other side is the negative. It is a continuum. At any point, we may say, more is positive and less is negative. Thus we live, each in one's own world, but all sharing all categories; far and near, tall and short, bright and dark, hard and soft, rich and poor, beautiful and ugly, love and hatred, generous and greedy, calm and disturbed, fast and slow, attraction and repulsion, happiness and sorrow, saintly and sinful. (Blonde and brunette?)

At any point, in any context, any statement is relative, because life functions only in duality. The sensing mind takes its conditional stand. There can be no absoluteness ascribed to anything, for we exist in relativity. All our words have been framed by this limitation. Mind's name is relativity and it needs words denoting pairs of opposites (even electrons and protons, big bang and big crunch). But when the mind collectively groups all opposites into one basket labeled RELATIVITY, it must posit an otherness as its valid opposite, and that opposite emerges as the word (concept) ABSOLUTE. Now the mind can relax comfortably, and not feel deprived or defeated. Never mind that this absolute is no absolute, being an off-spring of relativity!

The relative mind can indulgently wink at its own cleverness and drag the "absolute" from an unreachable 'beyond' into its own sphere(as a monkey may adopt a man?), but to believe that thereby it has ascended from comparison to consummation, would be a vain pretence and a pit-fall.

Therefore the sagacity of Sanskrit language would only say "not two"; it would not opt to say "only one". When duality perishes, the number game is abandoned. It has died a natural death. Duality extended is plurality and the setting is linearity. When that function itself is falsified – as 'seen' by the 'seer' – 'one' has no meaning as a word or a concept. That mental space has been erased. We, you and I, in the dualistic mode of relativity, if called upon to apply our minds to unitary transcendence (another word, how else?) will summon to our rescue (and survival) such words as Reality, Self-realization, Enlightenment, Liberation or Salvation. We like to believe for our intellectual comfort that this is absolute. At the same time the uncompromising loyalty of the scientist to observation, experiment and measurement declares, and honestly has to declare, that the point of absoluteness cannot be obtained through the reduction or extension of progressive process. In heat, absolute zero is unattainable. In work, perpetual motion is not even a notion. In entropy, the maximum cannot be reached. In the solid rock there is no stillness, only atomic whirlpools.

Then where shall we locate and how identify the Truth of this thought that is entrenched in the mind and wears the aura of being the consummation of the saga of science that has progressed from determinism to relativity to quantum probability, but as "Absolute" is yet evasive, teasing and taunting as the hidden Unified Field of energy or the Theory of Everything, avoiding capture in the net of a single equation that would hold good for all the forces that are themselves the foundation of cosmic existence?

Time and space deceived us posing as two absolutes, a patent contradiction right there, and were only recently welded into a continuum. "Time passes" we all believed; and fooling us thus time passed and we failed! Time is an interval between two events. Time is a unit of measure, be it an instant or an aeon. Therefore time begins at the second event when the first *measurable interval* comes into being. So if it is natural to the scientist to say "Time began with the big bang", the statement is correct with reference to our perception of time, but to call the bang *'the'* singularity of the creative impulse must be an error, because the first cause must have preceded it and remained, shall we say, unknown (unknowable) to time. But how? Because at the first event time was a concept of time, not a measure of time. And time does not exist to science except as a measure. Then, where, how, or in whom or what, was conceptual time, that potency, that seed-state that was yet to sprout? That indeed is, and should be the question. The question of First Cause does not relate to the first billionth second, for that too is an interval. That cause was before time.

We attribute concept to a mind. Science rightly admits no mind outside time. The equation of the Unified Field must unravel this riddle, or accept that equations can only equate and with what can one-without-a-second be equated? Time for a breathing pause ........

Relaxing in the break with light-hearted levity, yet not losing the gravity (say that again?) of our probe, permit me this rhymed homage to Einstein.

# WANTED: SPACE FOR TIME

*Einstein, his bushy eye-brows furrowed with thought,*
*Contemplated the clinching answer that he sought.*
*"Time till now has been the great imposter*
*That now deserves unmasking and ouster.*
*It is high time I put TIME in its proper place,*
*Eureka! Squeeze time into all of SPACE!*
*Henceforth time shall be space's fourth dimension,*
*Though some may find it hard for comprehension.*
*It is quite simple if you stop being primitive;*
*Time is not absolute, it is only relative."*

# "Save Me, God" or "Save Me, Gravity"?

When God is not totally denied as an impossibility, or dismissed as an absurdity, how does the word-concept GOD unfold in the scientific mind? If it denotes the ultimate unified field of all energies, "as well as consciousness" as Bhaumik hedges (hesitantly?), are we holding an assemblage or a seamless fusion? Is consciousness fundamentally constituted in our understanding on the same parameters as other energies, or is there a quantum gap? Consciousness is experienced in oneself, saint or scientist, and is the indelible factor for knowledge of things. Whatever is identified by sound (name) and shape (form) is a "thing". Be it forces like gravity and electromagnetic radiation, be it objects like earth and the sun, we do not bestow self-consciousness on them. They know not themselves (or me), whereas surely I know them. That is to say consciousness knows them. Therein seems to be a quaint or mysterious angle (beyond science's geometry) to this factor. Which sets me musing. When in trouble or distress or pain or confusion most of us tend to turn the mind to "God". But no one ever prays to gravity or electromagnetic radiation. I will wager that even Newton and Maxwell did not. The consciousness in me with an instinct for self-preservation admits the universal consciousness, posits in it a reachable relationship in real terms, and therefore invokes the higher potential of what is already possessed in lesser measure. Instinct seems to sense an inherent kinship and trust it.

If walking in the hills I suddenly slip precariously, the inadvertent exclamation is "My God!", not "My Gravity!". Science may gag me on both counts, but shortlist me for a Nobel prize if I had shouted "My neurons!" In that moment of crisis, when time-sequenced reason cannot articulate, my nature turns to a supremacy that, by implication, is present and knowing and can (if it so wills) respond and intercede. By the same implication, Mr. Gravity, though present, knows not and therefore, kind though he be, cannot respond. Mr. Gravity is acting on my body but cannot react to my mind. Why this premonition that, may be, Mr. God can?

If you do not mind (this word will not leave us!), let us be entertained (then enlightened) by this limerick (author unknown to me) :

There was a young man who said, "God,
To you it must seem very odd,
That a tree as a tree
Simply ceases to be
When there is no one about in the quad."

*And God replied:*
"Young man, your astonishment is odd,
I'm always about In the quad
And that's why the tree
Never ceases to be
As observed by yours faithfully, God"

The essence of it is not different from the Zen koan which asks "When a huge tree crashes in the depths of an uninhabited mountain, does the fall make a noise?" After a pause (not idly to sip tea) return to the dictum that says *inter alia* that what is not known to exist does not exist. Do not rush to rebuke angrily "you mean to say..." because the seers did not mean to say what you mean to say they meant to say! Words can be used differently. We shall, for the present, forsake habit and listen with an open mind.

Mind is consciousness in movement. The energy is of Consciousness, the moved blocks are thoughts (quanta of knowledge?), and mind is the field. From where is the talk of energy fields arising? Not in gravity. Gravity knows not its existence. The talk arises in consciousness, in mind's energy field that is self-aware, and *therefore* capable of being aware of all fields. If one word, one concept, one recognized reality shall have priority here by right of inheritance, is it not *consciousness?*

And yet science says our consciousness (which itself made the discoveries) is a product or epi-phenomenon of brain, which is molecules put together by Time and Chance, the molecules reducible to sub-atomic particles, in turn reducible to energy fields, the fields having no consciousness, of course. Of course, or off course?

Many an eminent scientist has not escaped these questions within himself. Max Planck said "I regard consciousness as primary. I regard matter as derivative of consciousness". Arthur Eddington said "All through the physical world runs that unknown content that must surely be the stuff of our consciousness". Schrodinger and Heisenberg were convinced that there was a "before" to the "beginning", a beyond to energy-filled space. John Wheeler wants the concept of observer changed to a "participator". Fritjof Capra and Ken Wilber seem inclined the same way. So is Mani Bhaumik, whose hesitant concurrence (in "Code name God") has prompted me to shape these thoughts.

Bhaumik writes "We have established *opportunity*" Agreed –

after all, Time provides it to patience that can wait a billion years. "We have identified the means". Agreed – after all, chance can create any configuration, given time. Did not some one say that out of a million monkeys tapping the keys of a million type-writers (monkeys can't yet handle computers) for a million years, one of them may produce a sonnet? Then Bhaumik writes "But we are missing the motive". Agreed again. But why does scientific rationality fight shy at this point? "Motive" belongs to conscious thinking ; call it will, call it intelligence, even call it intent or indul-gence, all expressions which are facets of consciousness. But then, as long as you insist on matter (brain) being the source of consciousness, what is this talk of "motive" in understanding the origin of creation? Can matter have a motive? Inevitably, centered in this faulted conclusion, science knows almost everything about the content in creation but nothing about the intent therein.

"With the startling assertion of new physics", writes Bhaumik, "science was tip-toeing to the threshold of spirituality". A happy consummation to be devoutly (or electronically) wished for, but it will not happen. Not with this mental block which blocks the mind's origin itself; not while science amazingly persists with the contradiction that inert brain-cells constituted of matter produce consciousness which is the light of knowledge, the animation of the brain and the body. Where, then, is the road ahead? Therefore the tip-toeing scientist will stand on the threshold, may even prepare to knock on the door, but will mumble to himself "I have made a mistake. I have come to the wrong address", and quickly retreat. So near and *yet* so far!

And, in his own way, he will be correct. He will be true to himself and his frame of enquiry, which is relativity, linearity, continuity, connectivity. Viewed in those terms, the threshold reached would seem to be non-space for a foot-fall, non-time for a step forward, non-energy for any movement. It would be, in familiar feel and phrase, nothing (no-thing), void, zero. That is when the mind, deceived because of its own false expectations and evaluations, would feel, as in Bhaumik's beautiful sigh of melancholy, "Behind all the fine draperies, there is no longer anybody home". But the owner was always home. It was the shadow that stood at the door, giving itself a false reality and declaring the real person's assumed absence. The relative denies the Absolute because it has credited itself with wholeness.

All the time, or timelessly, that for which we framed the word God, which is reality beyond relativity, which is Absolute Consciousness, has been inseparably one with us. The Eternal Presence can only remonstrate : Tip-toeing towards Me? No need. I am Myself toe-tipping towards you, touching you which is more than what you can do to Me. My children, I have been gently stepping on your toes always, but you refuse to recognize Me. I am in you as the cognizing consciousness of your five senses; the touch (on your toes too), the sight, the smell, the hearing, the tasting. Your total knowledge has been derived through the five sense-organs, no more, no less. Their inputs collectively constitute your mind. I am in you. Look in your consciousness and find Me. If you run or tip-toe *out* there, the search can only end in a void. (I will be there too, but not available to your vision.)

Where is the missed cue in the brilliance of scientific enquiry, in the collective intelligence of a procession of men of genius, in the meticulous adherence to observation, experiment and reconfirmation, that science could have got it wrong? Science does not claim that science has got it all today – it concedes that it still needs a tomorrow. Scientists only protest that if philosophers mean to say others had it yesterday and that was not even on a parallel track... then tell your story to the deaf, says science. Feathers are ruffled unnecessarily. Please unplug and listen. In cosmic creation, as in a game of hide and seek, there was a hiding, but in the spirit of fun signs and symbols were deliberately left scattered in the scene, to facilitate the chase and assure discovery. Been a boy-scout? Well, you still are, if you have preserved your enthusiasm.

Whatever or whoever created the cosmos did not leave a wholesome ready-to-view picture of its origin or evolution but left some clues. Such a picture was cut into many, zigzag bits and pieces which were strewn across the expanses of time and space. That was the gift that the mind of man received on attaining the adult-age of enquiry; enquiry beyond the problems of the temporal, into the depths of the infinite. The collective intelligence of material scientists has laboriously put together the pieces of the jig-saw puzzle, and a picture is emerging, but a problem is already discernable. The emerging picture seems to be near completion but it holds no promise of revealing the origin. Missing pieces are yet being searched out and slotted into the picture, but as yet there are no clues about the donor of this challenging jig-saw puzzle. When all the pieces are in place, there will be a picture, but it will not be the picture that science labored to complete. *When the task is completed the origin of creation would still evade definition.* The picture would resemble reality, yet be deficient and therefore unreal. It might unravel creative *evolution,* but will not reveal the creator (whoever or whatever). Effects of energy-play will be sequentially aligned, but the first-cause will remain a mystery to science.

I may walk around the globe, but in doing so, where and when did I cross the horizon? No answer will emerge, because the question is posed in wrong terms. Earth and sky are perceived, the horizon is conceptualized. The eternal failure to cross the horizon is the transcendental revelation that linearity returns to its source and makes a circle of its long progress. That is the truth and nothing else. Words lose their outlines in the flux of finality.

To have believed that the determined scientific truth of 'creation' will spell out the truth of the 'creator' is flawed, but not foolish. Science must dispassionately evaluate the modified frame of enquiry. Entrenched in relativity, science cannot deny the absolute. Nor can it conveniently equate the two. A good clue for a re-think is proffered by the common, yet fantastic phenomenon of optical reflection. Images have appearance but no substance; seem to be in space but the space itself is not; seem distorted in curved reflecting surfaces, tinted in coloured ones, misty in smoked ones. There will be simultaneously a hundred images of the one-and- only subject if it is surrounded by a hundred mirrors. The unmoving subject is seen shaking if the mirrors are shaken. Exact replication is denied by lateral inversion.

Cosmic relativity needs to be assessed from this angle also. Legitimate questions will arise: What Is the "mirror" in cosmic terms? What is it made of? And, inevitably (back to square one), who made it? The field of reference must shift from finding to feeling, from outer observation to inner introspection. For a start, let me re-study the oft-experienced dream phenomenon. My dream is a reflection of my total mind. I, in my dream, am a reflection of myself, and all the others in the dream are also reflections of my mind which is myself. I must look for the answers in myself. Where my dream is "relative", I (this person) am the contiguous Absolute Cause. Where I (creation) am relative, what would be the contiguous Absolute Cause? That, de-coded, is God. This is the point of the jig-saw puzzle; (i) Creation is relativity; divided and therefore limited, qualified and quantified; (ii) First uncaused cause must be Absolute, beyond all terms of relativity (time, space, causality); (iii) Our personal minds correspond to *reflected consciousness* (which defines man, change, becomings); (iv) God would be our word for Absolute Consciousness (Pure Being).

The self-awareness of personal consciousness has the inherent potential to take the I-am-ness beyond the mirror, beyond relativity to Reality. Within, not out there. Science journeys only out there. Science is walking the endless millenniums of time, and time is its measure of energy functions. But deep at the centre Time is not just a chime of a restive wall-clock, it is the key to the mystery of the Creator's secret lock.

Science has recognized that within energy-fields that pervade all space, objectification happens. The object only seems to stand apart; truly, *it itself is the field* – objects are seen as plural; field is unitary. Similarly, minds are plural; consciousness is unitary. The synonymity erroneously equating total consciousness and individual mind is the abyss in the rationale of science.

Words cannot change beyond words, and the last word must remain a word, even if it be the word SILENCE. The last word has the overtone of being the first word. That end of sound is, in reality, the source of sound. Know this too, and decide. The supreme Silence of the sage's stilled mind is not the silence of the grave-yard, it is life eternal.

Mind cognizing events creates time as a temporal link and moves from event to event. Time is the road that mind lays for itself to walk upon. The walker moves; can the road move? Time does not pass, it is only a passage. When mind stops, time ceases to be. Stilled time is killed time. But a stilled mind is one that is transformed from time-space conditioned "living" (a verb) to "Life" (a noun); from cosmic "becomings" to Timeless Being; from relative to Absolute; from reflection to Reality, from manifestation to the First Cause.

❦

# Four Forces, One Symmetry

New Age Science at its conciliatory best may grant that perhaps the experience of the mystics has an analogue in the "unbroken wholeness" of quantum physicists, but will regretfully add that "the greatest obstacle to reconciling science and spirituality has been the personification of God" (Bhaumik). On the contrary, I would say the sole obstacle is the failure of science to personify the "unbroken wholeness". Any number of force fields may be integrated through addition to arrive at an unbroken wholeness, but the totality has to be *known* to exist. The force fields are inert, singly or totally. Consciousness brings them into knowledge. Knowledge is personal and paramount. Thus consciousness translates to knower, and a knower is personal (you personally know that). The 'personal god' is a consolation prize given to mental man who sees himself as a conscious entity and cannot set apart existence from knowledge of such existence. That is *religion,* the devout way of living, wherein man (mind) interacts with his personal god (while the personal blonde is made to wait). *Spirituality* is more than interaction, it is integration; a quantum jump, a transcendence, where-after, who is there to personify what? Let those that insist there cannot be GOD with form, then concede that there can be no MIND without form (of things perceived). Then how shall all good people of the earth deal with this persistent word "GOD" and keep peace amongst themselves? By not making an issue of it. If a person enjoys happy intoxication daily by drinking out of an empty bottle, what is your problem with him? (The earlier chapter in this book on "The Wandering Minstrels, one lame, one blind" deserves your attention.)

The microcosmic and the macrocosmic are structured (conceived?) on the same basic parameters and that is why one Theory (fact?) of Everything must be possible. A circle assembled on all planes is the sphere, an atom enlarged is the cosmos, the energies and gyrations of particles are kin to those of the planets. For our contemplation when time permits: It seems the personal-I (ego) is not other than the cosmic-I (God). The creator is simultaneously the creature. Therefore I venture to say that the forces in the matterfield can be said to have identical counterparts in the mindfield. (What follows is, in rough outline, my way of perceiving the facets. Let us say, herein I am not asserting, but then, I am not apologizing either.) Physics enumerates four forces – gravity, electro-magnetic radiation, nuclear strong force, nuclear weak force.

Gravity determines the relative positioning of all bodies of matter, their configuration in space, for instance the sun and our own earth, their orbits, their collisions, their destiny as it were. That word "destiny", when felt at the mental level (the sun and the earth refusing to have any feelings), becomes *Karma*, a much used and much maligned indicator for the occurrence of events. Poor karma, it is only the unchanging unerring causal determinant that functions as the event-manager in mentation, just like gravity in material creation. That these words are now entering your mental space is as much the only and inevitable resolution of causal correctness, as the fact that the earth can only be in the space it is occupying now. Thoughts, which are mental bodies, *gravitate* according to the laws of force of the energy of consciousness. As we think, so we act. As we act, the events of our lives are structured. That much for gravity. It is the sensed result of energy fulfilling itself in manifestation. Karma is the manifesting law of causal correctness in physical connectivity, moved by the energy of consciousness. Gravity is the law behind waves in the ocean of space; karma is the law behind waves in the ocean of consciousness.

Next we come to electromagnetic radiation, which is the energy-ocean filling the space-ocean, not two entities, but one "field". We would say "Why, space should be empty", but there is no such reality as "empty space". A void does not exist. Space, time and field are inseparable. A field is a physical state of space itself, and space does not exist without a field. Reality has been revisited by this knowledge. The knowledge was not revealed as a Christmas gift by this energy or by space. It was a configuration in the consciousness (knowledge-potential) of the scientist. Call it intelligence, genius, intuition ; you are saying big, bigger, biggest. Intuition is when steps of intellectual reasoning are by-passed in a surge of vaulting to the peak. It is this intelligence-mode of consciousness that pervades all of creation. As observed, electromagnetic radiation is the authority over space, but not really. That is only vassal to the monarch, who is consciousness, the observer, the knower. Space is filled with other energy-fields, but space itself, with the fields, is a content of consciousness. Let us get the priority right.

Third, there is the strong nuclear force, astoundingly stronger than gravity or electromagnetism, but which comes into reckoning only when we move from peering through the telescope at cosmos, to scrutiny of the atom through the microscope. This is the force that keeps positively charged protons together (not repelled) and gives rise to hundreds of individual atoms from light-hearted hydrogen to ominous uranium and beyond, collectively creating our world and the stars. This is equitable to the ego-sense in consciousness, science's ghost-in-the machine, the i-am-ness of each individual. It is the memory power that integrates the person, the adhesive for the bits of life's progressive experiences to be held coherently as the personality. It is the glue that binds passing events into abiding memory. Without it, who is any "I" ?

Fourth and final, there is weak nuclear force, nomenclature "weak" only because its influence is limited to inconceivably miniscular range, even though this weak force is billions of times stronger than gravity. This force governs the rate and process of radioactive decay within the nucleus. It has a fundamental role in the nuclear activity of the solar furnace that provides life-sustaining energy upon our globe. This weak force which is not weak will stand equated to the mind in meditation, when all the energy of mental consciousness is focused upon itself and the ego-person who stands out in the "field" as a "thing", objectified and observed, dissolves into the observing consciousness. This is the culminating aspect of energy-play. It is the first fundamental and the last. It is the force that separates the inseparable and unites the undivided. Meditation is radiation where elimination spells enhancement. The seeming interaction is between the personal ego and the totality of consciousness. "Ego" signifies the personal sense of being, the I-am-ness of the individual, the conscious-thing. But consciousness in totality is cosmic, and its self-awareness cannot admit otherness. Therefore, what is "interaction" here? Where is the space for such? Even Plank's measure here would become zero. This is the state of realization or self-actualization, and this potency is also inherent in conscious energy.

Thus all forces and fields that science has so brilliantly recognized are not contrary, not even different, but are truly unified, and that unity is consciousness. All this quantifying, qualifying, categorizing and measuring – and finally equating – is taking place in relativity. The consciousness we have here analyzed and synthesized, likewise belongs to relativity. It shares the relative reality of creation – more accurately, it is the support. In this manifestation it is not Reality.

The chapter on "Images and Illusions" brings the relevance of this understanding as a factor that should not be left out of scientific evaluation. The mind is the ladder, consciousness is the climber. When the climbing ends, the climber ceases, not by negation but by quantum elevation – and that is Absolute Consciousness. Nothing and everything. Zero energy and unified energy field. Can space be termed a climber when there is nowhere for it to climb into? Only me, located and limited in space, can think of climbing and climbers.

In "Code name God" the author writes about nature's "symmetries", which is not about art or aesthetics but about quantum physics. "The forces and fields we know are the result of broken symmetries of nature. So, restoration of symmetries is the magic key to unification, and unification is the key to understanding the common source".

The parallel has been stated in the idiom of consciousness also. As I have said before, whatever is true of force fields must be true, even more accurately true, of the energy of consciousness. See them together, and you truly see. Otherwise there is no seeing, no knowing; only misapprehension.

Manifested consciousness, experienced as the personal mind, is analytically seen as three distinguishable aspects; as "water" is more fully understand by knowing ice, liquid, and vapor. The three aspects are called (in Sanskrit) Gunas; they are 1) *Sattva Guna* with attributes of purity, tranquility, whiteness etc. 2) *Rajo Guna*, dynamic, energetic, red etc. 3) *Tamo Guna*, dull, agitated, black etc. In our individual functioning minds, each one of us is an admixture of these three qualities (or characters), the proportions varying from man to man (even more from woman to woman?), and also from time to time in the same person. The three can be diagrammatically represented as three lines of force converging upon a point which is the instant mind. Each line, with its length and angle of impact will signify the force it imparts to the point. The resultant of the three forces (three arrows) will be the vector resolved in direction and momentum. That will precisely determine where the mind will land the next moment in terms of its quality, quantity and direction. The lack of symmetry in the three arrows, changing but not ending, ensures that the personality is never at rest. No one else need be blamed or blessed, as the personal causal sequence is the fuel driving the person.

This is not an essay on philosophy, but I have had to say (briefly, you will agree) this much about "gunas", to establish that when the three arrows acting on a point are in equilibrium, then, in spite of an on-going energy play, there is dynamic stillness in the point of their focus. That, I submit, is the restoration of symmetry. Look for the "common source" in that state of mind which is stilled by meditation, when thought-waves generated by conflicting gunas have subsided due to perfect balance and not a ripple breaks the tranquil surface of the ocean of consciousness.

Scientist and Sage, the two words are next to each other in my dictionary. How to return to the source? should be the question. The quest is not to see the source, but to possess it. That is the jack-pot, not the few coins spilled. Potential must be rightly seen, manifestation is only a step away. See what is abundantly expressed through Nature, even in the plant kingdom. Order comes out of intelligence, chaos out of its absence. Out of the miscellany of the compounds in the soil of the earth, the plant functions with recognition, organization, and exactitude, synthesizing colour, fragrance, symmetry and flavor into flower, branch, and fruit. It grows purposefully from sapling to a mighty tree. And as the crowning glory of all the effort, intuitively puts itself, all of itself, faithfully, into its own tiny seed. Science is questing for the universal law when it seeks the unified field. The scientist discovers what he discovers through intellect. The "sage" is the one who creates space through intuition. And thereby vaults over a forbidden fence. At the end of the day, the scientist manifests genius; the seer, luminance. The potential denies nothing, gifts nothing. The Law-maker is the Law. These two, which are not two, appear to the mind of man as Personal God and Impersonal God.

I have said it before, I will say it again: Science cannot reach God, the Scientist can.

If David Bohm conceptualized "something exceeding zero" and named it the implicate order, was it not the same as the assertion of Vedanta that the mind's "zero" is not without content, and exceeding it would mean zeroing the zero? Which is, transcending the limits of the mind? There he was right. If Bohm went on to say that "mental reality and consciousness are projections from this implicate order", is it not (- or, is it?) tantamount to saying that, at the source, is Absolute Consciousness, the Reality and mind and matter are at best a relative reality (a polite word for non-reality), like reflections? Some high thinkers of these days (being, in all senses, high-fliers) have snidely said "God is dead". Nodding to each other they confirm that Artificial Intelligence and cloned creations attended the funeral. Indeed?

Your computer's artificial intelligence has 0 and 1 for its baggage. Original intelligence (mind) has zero (concept) for its baggage. Only God, the zeroed zero, is without baggage. So much for science. So little for God.

❧

# God's Address
## House Number Zero,
### Infinity Road, Creation

Please do not lapse into sympathy for God. So little for God? It is truer to say, nothing for God. Zero signifies the deepest conceptualization and the perfected symbolism of higher mathematics. Zero is irreducible and yet it is functional by itself. Bhaumik says: "Zero is invariably connected to infinity. Could zero as easily stand as the source of *everything* as the realm of *nothing*?" See the natural flow of words from which there is no escape – every-*thing* and no-*thing*. Mind must live with its words, the two co-exist; there is no mind without thoughts, there are no thoughts without words. Things are known, and knowing is the sole realm of consciousness. That potential does not belong to matter. Our mind has embedded for us the phrase "light of knowledge". The illumination of knowledge is obviously not the lighting up of a thing. We need optical light to be able to see a thing, but a lighted object is not known, that is to say sense perceived, unless the light of consciousness enwraps it. The inherited First Declaration "Let there be light" sanctions the movement of Consciousness and not of optical light, be it of an oil-lamp or a laser beam. Light of the sun cannot see the world, unless the light of Consciousness "sees" the sun. If darkness envelops the world, vision is lost but not *sight*. Consciousness cannot go blind. It sees the darkness and you say "it is dark" because the light of consciousness is cognizing darkness, the same way it cognized lighted objects. The five senses we possess, sight, hearing, smell, taste and touch, are attributes of consciousness, and are of individual function through the instrumentality of eye, ear, nose, tongue and skin; the collective function is vested in the mind through the instrumentality of brain. Let us not mix up energies and equipments. Sense-organs, nerves, brain – that is the mechanical device. Where is energy in this?

A quantum is a small unit in which energy may express itself. A quantum of light is a photon. Science says that "the magnitude of energy of a quantum field is not continuous but discrete or quantized". Then, it is not unscientific to say that a quantum of consciousness is a thought. (The reference is to "reflected consciousness" or mentation, because under discussion here is human experience of the relativistic world of relative reality.) Thoughts are intermittent. Each thought is an elementary particle born out of the underlying quantum field of consciousness. It rises in the field, has its brief existence in terms of space-time, and sinks into the field. The individual ego-sense (the personalized consciousness) is a construct of knower-knowing-known, the same as subject-energy-object. The rapid recurrence of this phenomena creates the semblance of unbroken occurrence, like a flaming torch, twirled rapidly, appears as a ring of fire.

At this event horizon of motionless (mindless) Absolute Consciousness exploding into thought-process (mind) to bring into being relativity of interactions, what was the source, the Uncaused Cause, the state of pre-space-time?

We are looking to right and left searching for Reality; on one side, at the conclusions of scientific observations (proved outside); on the other side at experience of conscious consolidation (known inside). The scientific researcher can prove his findings to another, but the sage can only indicate his experience and invite, even initiate, the other to move into the same experience, but it has to be done by that other one, for himself – and the explosion would then be into silence, the expansion would then be into stillness. All these are contradictions in words. And that is why dialogue or discourse upon the science-philosophy border turns so vexatious. There, it is easier said than done. So far, it has been often said, seldom done. Yet, the effort must go on.

Explaining "Inflationary Theory" of Alan Guth, Bhaumik says in "Code name God": "Mathematical analysis shows that the sum total of positive energy in the universe *equals* the sum total of negative energy. Therefore, strange as it may sound, the total energy of the universe is zero". He goes on to ask how this huge universe can have zero energy sustaining it, and hints at a plausible answer: "It can, if the energy of inflation arose from something else, something with a value of zero."

Now, let us turn our attention to the other side. (Please, I am not talking of opposite sides, only the other side, two of them placed side by side. The final resolution will have to be that there is unity, not by addition of separate entities, but by clear recognition that one *includes* the other, and *exceeds* the limitations of the other.) In a Hindu scriptural classic aged beyond dating, known as "Isa Upanishad", an invocatory verse precedes the crisp and brief text. The verse translates into:

(⁵)"That is Whole; this is Whole; from the Whole the Whole becomes manifest. From the Whole when the Whole is negated what remains is again the Whole."

---

*(5) In 1991, seeking answers about creation and created, straying into the no man's land between science and philosophy, I gathered my contemplations into "The Physics of Karma (A requiem to Time.)" Then this verse revealed its relevance to the vexed equations. I wrote a short article and placed it in my book as an appendix, without intrusion on the rigid rationale of less adventurous readers!*

That and this are the two words used, and they denote in our usage the farthest and the nearest. As the two extremities of linearity, they signify the end and the beginning, the infinity and the zero. The vision of the sage would be terribly squint-eyed to the scientific optician, unless… unless the two "quantities" are IDENTICAL and their symbols interchangeable. Zero zeroed should equal infinity, and infinity should be wholly swallowed by zero.

Physicist Michilo Kaku has said that of all theories "the silliest is quantum theory.. but it is unquestionably correct!" Einstein has agreed, saying "The more success the quantum theory has, the sillier it looks!" Bhaumik, the Indian village kid turned American super-scientist, with his precocious half-inherited half-imported genes, says haltingly, yet hopefully, that… "We may … perhaps… have seen (through quantum weirdness) a faint glimmering of the nature of God… of the cosmos arising from an address numbered zero." May I say, the address is being correctly heard, but is being noted down with wrong symbols? – so much so, the equations will be returned with a cosmic postal stamp: Cannot locate addressee.

The quoted scriptural equation says it correctly by not using words to make a direct statement but by making the words collide and perish in a surge of self-contradiction, simultaneously promoting limited meaning into limitless experience. Zeroed God expended zero energy to "create" this zero cosmos. So what happened? Nothing happened. At the most, mind happened to itself, and the cosmos happened to the mind. Mind is available to us. God is not. Mind is our laboratory. Hold consciousness answerable. But if we ourselves imprison consciousness in the matter frame of brain cells, God help us. Or (damn it all!) God help Himself.

ॐ

# THE SEVENTH HILL-TOP

The eminent scientist in Mani Bhaumik reveals deep insight when he says: "The field of endeavor I know best is laser physics, and… it has offered me a superb metaphor for the state of mind we are seeking". Beautiful. We have not only a simile of inert cosmic energy and conscious and personal energy, we also have the simile of optic light and the light of knowledge. Coherence, perfect phase, and reinforcement are the key words in both planes. Photons are marshalled in one, thoughts are marshalled in the other. But, sir, why are you still leaning so heavily on "neurological accuracy", on the studies on prefrontal lobes, and synapses, pariet functions, and EEG readings? These terms refer to the brain which is the equipment, not to consciousness whose energy is life, knowledge and self-aware existence. An equipment is only a necessary adjunct for energy to manifest – as a bulb to electricity – and must be parked in its allotted slot. You are speaking so well about physics and philosophy, about energy fields and consciousness, but you are hedging on the ONE ONLY, and would like to see two of them shaking hands. What gain would it be if you and your shadow shook hands? What kind of a party?

The impossibility of it was brusquely stated (and you have quoted it approvingly) by Meister Eckhart: "Get out of the way and let God be God in you." Man thinks he is the owner of the brain; and consciousness, at best, a slavish tenant! In truth, that which can be called God is the sole owner, and you called man, are not even a tenant. You are the shadow. Imagine your shadow claiming tenancy rights in your house, if not ownership! Bhaumik, a real estate mogul, should be relieved and gratified to know that the original owner of space (God) began with a tenancy problem (relativity) and it is still not resolved (because the scientist is the magistrate). What wonder that the same problem is the bane of the propertied, world-wide!

You, Bhaumik, have written "I owned six hill-top houses, with million dollar hill-top views". I rejoice with you, I have read how you stood up since boyhood till you got finally counted. Enjoy the six. Indian mythology (hiding its deeper significances) says the seventh peak is heaven. Do not stop going up; get there. And there, as earlier, you will realize that you have arrived at one more bubble, for, heaven – include hell, but do not book a room there – is also only sensed perceptions, like everything else now; more intense, that is all. It too is in the frame of relativity. Leave the poets to idly fantasize that the world is a bubble, leave the luxury of soap-bubbles to the blondes in the bathtub, but you, with a laser mind, burst the bubble and enter the space within, and stay quiet – oh! so blissfully quiet – till all of space enters you. The I-ness. The Aloneness.

My thrust throughout this book, supplement included, has been to persuade the scientific temper to see the one gap that is preventing the linearity of its knowledge from becoming the circle of its conclusion. I will leave you with the words of two sages, so recent that the echoes of their voices are vibrating amongst us.

**Nisargadatta Maharaj (1897 to 1981)**
Look at the mind as a function of matter, and you have

science. Look at matter as the product of the mind, and you have religion.

**Bhagavan Ramana Maharshi (1879 to 1950)**

(Dialogue no.11 and no.12 from "Chapter II; Spiritual Instruction", in "Collected works of Ramana Maharshi", a Ramanashram Publication)

(Readers will carefully note that psychic nerves are not known to physical anatomy, the "Heart" is not the cardiac organ but a "power-centre", and the Self is the same as Absolute Consciousness).

*Question:* How do the triple factors (i.e knower, known and knowledge), which are absent in deep sleep, samadhi, etc., manifest themselves in the Self (in the states of waking and dreaming)?

*Answer:* From the Self there arise in succession:

(i) *Chidabhasa* (reflected consciousness) which is a kind of luminosity.

(ii) *Jiva* (the individual consciousness) or the seer or the first concept.

(iii) Phenomena, that is the world.

*Question:* Since the Self is free from the notions of knowledge and ignorance how can it be said to pervade the entire body in the shape of sentience or to impart sentience to the senses?

*Answer:* Wise men say that there is a connection between the source of the various psychic nerves and the Self, that this is the knot of the Heart, that the connection between the sentient and the insentient will exist until this is cut asunder with the aid of true knowledge, that just as the subtle and invisible force of electricity travels through wires and does many wonderful things, so the force of the Self also travels through psychic nerves and, pervading the entire body, imparts sentience to the senses, and that if this knot is cut, the Self will remain as it always is, without any attributes.

*From "Talks with Sri Ramana Maharshi" - 15th Oct. 1938*

*Question:* What is *svarupa* (form) and *arupa* (formless) of the mind?

*Maharshi:* When you wake up from sleep a light appears, that is the light of the Self passing through *Mahat Tattva*. It is called cosmic consciousness. This is *arupa*. The light falls on the ego and is reflected therefrom. Then the body and the world are seen. This mind is *svarupa*. The objects appear in the light of this reflected consciousness. This light is called *jyoti*.

*Explanatory comment:*

Everything that the sage speaks - the Realized person, the Enlightened one, the Liberated one, are also our words to denote and distinguish the transcendental attainment of the Sage - is spoken out of experience, and not out of theory, logical extension, or learnt and remembered knowledge. We know the words, of course, but have not attributed to them the deeper, often unsuspected, intimations that they are capable of conveying to us when thus structured and empowered in the idiom that lifts relativity beyond its boundaries. That "beyond" is not added space – how can it be? – it is Absolute.

This brief reply from Ramana Maharshi is the answer to "How does the un-manifest manifest?" The scientist has the same question "How did creation start?" or "what triggered the Big Bang?" On this question the mind of science, bounded by time-space-coordinates, searches in a dark room for a black cat that is not there. Absolute consciousness (the science of mind-less-ness?), being Self-Aware in the Sage, effortlessly flows in the idiom of revelation. The answer remains present but hidden in everyone's daily life, like the car-key in your pocket that you are frantically searching for (more true of professors, unkind wits have said), and not finding. The instant contains the truth of eternity for the sage, but will deny it to him who begs Time for the gift of vision.

Here the Maharshi is focusing our attention on familiar territory, as intimate as our daily waking up from sleep. To our easy understanding, sleep is the un-manifest state of one's consciousness, and waking up is bringing the world into manifestation through sensed recognition by the resurrected ego-I. We have to understand the teaching in personal terms, and also extrapolate it into a pre-personal context.

We are told there is the first instant in the transition from sleep into awakening, when a light manifests. This is the implication in "God said : Let there be Light." This kinetic energy (shakti) "passes through *Mahat Tattva*" which signifies the nascent seed potential of matter and mind (cosmos). It is now called "cosmic consciousness", because it has been moded into a generative thought. The creative momentum has been generated. But creation is not yet articulated. Therefore it is *"arupa"*, formless.

Next, the One Self assumes a plurality of nodal points, like one sun reflecting in a thousand pools of water to become a thousand suns. Each of these individualized focal points of consciousness is the "ego". The light of Total Consciousness "falls on the ego and is reflected therefrom". It is this reflected light that reveals "the body and the world"; and that is creation, perception, manifestation, *svarupa*. This sensing consciousness, with the personalized ego as its centre and support, is the "mind". Mind and time co-exist, because the content of mind is objects (things and events) and objects can only exist in time and space.

Thus, at journey's end, if science wants to proclaim "There is no matter, only energy", philosophy agrees and says more precisely "There is no *creation of universe,* only consciousness". But if science wants to access vistas of time and space, and chronicle the evolution of protons and molecules, of planets and galaxies, philosophy will gladly concede the relative reality and offer this sequence of creation. Ego-cognition and cosmic existence are coeval and co-terminal.

In the noble pursuit of Truth, scientists and philosophers are too genuine to engage in conflict without communication or dissent without discourse. The fulfillment is not through reconciliation but through resolution. The persisting dichotomy is because science is cerebral, while philosophy is mental. Let us go beyond the dictionary. Permit me to provoke a review: The two words, far from being synonyms, are exactly one cosmos apart because the cosmic world of matter is not the source of the cosmic mind. Cerebral; read brain. Mental; read consciousness.

## TO THE READER:

In this book I have deliberately attempted to be brief and concise, because two of my earlier books deal more expansively on thoughts and themes that have a bearing on the present work. I have avoided repetition. The need for this book arose basically to bridge first, and finally merge, what may seem to be different spheres of enquiry, physics and biology, when they turn to cosmic creation. The two books are:

### I. *The Physics Of Karma: (A Requiem To Time)*

Karma is the causal rightness in all events and sequences in creation. Karma is the operating law of the energy of Total Consciousness. It is one stream, one movement, engulfing all of cosmic creation. It is the core methodology of all forces playing on the material universe, and the mental universe. Karma includes all the physical laws defined by time, space and causation, and establishes the identical laws at work on the mental plane. Absolute Consciousness then reveals its transcendental supremacy as the source, the Absolute. The workings of Karma can be unraveled by every one of us in terms of our daily life. No. of Pages: 178 Price: Rs. 250

### II. *Death Was Never Born, Life Never Died: (Reincarnation Or Evolution?)* Earlier Title: *Birth, Play And Finale Of Mind*

Total Consciousness, absolute, undivided, eternal, is the source, the Reality. (Another word for it is God). In creation it is within the experience of each one of us as MIND. Mind is an illusory distorted presentation of Pure Consciousness, now seen as a dim reflection in a flawed mirror. That is the personal – you and me. Cosmic existence and experience is the voyage of desire, action, and reaction, till the error of limitation is overcome. The finale is the return to perfection. (Enlightenment, Realization, are other words for it.) This book investigates and examines evolution, "life-after-death", reincarnation, memory, sub-conscience, et al, and peeps over the horizon at Transcendence. Darwinism and Vedanta are analysed on merits of rationality.

The present reader, if so motivated, may consider referring to these books for more information. No. of Pages: 248 Price: Rs. 350

## OTHER BOOKS BY THE SAME AUTHOR:

*III. Can God Improve My Balance-Sheet? (Invoking The Inner Potential)*

A book of Business Management Psychology, self-management included (rather, self first.) It tells you how the true analysis and understanding of the psychology of desire, demand, action and reaction within oneself can create a harmony that invokes the inner potential of oneself. That brings success. Price: Rs. 350

*IV. Rising Sun, Melting Mists: (Knowledge Of Self Dispels Ignorance)* Earlier Title: *Whispers Heard Within*

A collection of brief articles, devotional/mystic, contemplative, and narrative. Sharp and crisp essays with a common thread of sincerity and intense spiritual aspiration. No. of Pages: 222 Price: Rs. 300

*V. Gentle Breeze, Rustling Leaves (Sing, My Soul, Your Symphony Of Silence)*

Gentle breezes blow across the mind, caressing the leaves of contemplation, emotion and wonder. The ego and the companion-self are in intimate conversation. Slowly the winds rest in space, the rustling sounds sink into silence. No. of Pages: 214 Price: Rs. 250

### *Vi. Diving Deep (Into Ramana Maharshi's Teachings)*

Spiritual seekers often glimpse the nature of Reality. They see sparks of truth but the goal is reached only when the fire of wisdom burns ignorance to ashes. Bhagavan Ramana Maharshi abides in Transcendence. Who can guide us better? But mere hearing is not the same as listening. Staring is not the same as seeing. We need to dive deep into His teachings. Pearls do not float on the surface. No. of Pages: 136 Price: Rs. 200

*Enquiries or Orders to: info@zenpublications.com*